FINDING THE NEXT STEVE JOBS

HOW TO FIND, KEEP,
AND NURTURE CREATIVE TALENT

NOLAN BUSHNELL
WITH GENE STONE

SIMON & SCHUSTER PAPERBACKS
New York London Toronto Sydney New Delhi

Simon & Schuster Paperbacks
A Division of Simon & Schuster, Inc.
1230 Avenue of the Americas
New York, NY 10020

First Simon & Schuster trade paperback edition September 2014

SIMON & SCHUSTER PAPERBACKS and colophon
are registered trademarks of Simon & Schuster, Inc.

For information about special discounts for bulk purchases,
please contact Simon & Schuster Special Sales at 1-866-506-1949
or business@simonandschuster.com.

The Simon & Schuster Speakers Bureau can bring authors to your
live event. For more information or to book an event contact the
Simon & Schuster Speakers Bureau at 1-866-248-3049 or visit our
website at www.simonspeakers.com.

Manufactured in the United States of America

10   9   8   7   6   5   4   3   2   1

Library of Congress Cataloging-in-Publication Data is available.

ISBN 978-1-4767-5981-4
ISBN 978-1-4767-5982-1 (pbk)
ISBN 978-1-4767-5983-8 (ebook)

For Steve Jobs and all the other creative people in my life

TABLE OF CONTENTS

I. Keeping and Nurturing the Next Steve Jobs

FINDING THE NEXT STEVE JOBS

INTRODUCTION

MAKE YOUR WORKPLACE AN ADVERTISEMENT
FOR YOUR COMPANY ADOPT FLEXIBLE PONGS
ADVERTISE CREATIVELY HIRE FOR PASSION
AND INTENSITY IGNORE CREDENTIALS LOOK
FOR HOBBIES USE EMPLOYEES AS RESOURCES
AVOID THE CLONES HIRE THE OBNOXIOUS HIRE
THE CRAZY FIND THE BULLIED LOOK FOR THE
LURKERS ASK ABOUT BOOKS SAIL A BOAT HIRE
UNDER YOUR NOSE COMB THROUGH TWEETS
VISIT CREATIVE COMMUNITIES BEWARE OF
POSEURS ASK ODD QUESTIONS CONDUCT DEEP
INTERVIEWS CELEBRATE INSTITUTE A DEGREE OF
ANARCHY PROMOTE PRANKSTERISM SKUNK IT
UP FOSTER FAIRNESS ISOLATE CHAMPION THE
BAD IDEAS CELEBRATE FAILURE REQUIRE RISK
REWARD TURKEYS MENTOR TREAT EMPLOYEES
AS ADULTS CREATE A CREATIVE CHAIN CREATE
A CREATIVE SPACE DESIGNATE A DEMO DAY
ENCOURAGE ADHD PRELOAD LEARN TO
TALK CREATIVE THINK TOYS NEUTRALIZE THE
NAYSAYERS WRITE DOWN OBJECTIONS TAKE
CREATIVESTOCREATIVEPLACESMAKESOMETHING
FOR THE RICH CHANGE EVERY DAY, EVERY
HOUR THROW THE DICE DUCK PROCESSES
TAKE A RANDOM WALK THROUGH WIKIPEDIA
DON'T COUNT ON ACCOUNTING INVENT
HAPHAZARD HOLIDAYS MIX IT UP GO TO SLEEP

C O N C L U S I O N

O

In 1980, business at my company, Chuck E. Cheese's, was thriving and I was feeling flush. So I bought a very large house on the Champ de Mars in Paris, right between the Eiffel Tower and the École Militaire. The home was quite amazing: At six stories, it spanned 15,000 square feet and featured marble staircases and a swimming pool in the basement. At the time, my wife and I didn't have any furniture, so we thought: Why not fill it up with people instead?

So we did. We threw a huge party, inviting everyone I knew at Chuck E. Cheese's and my other company, Atari, and all my old friends as well. Oddly, more people showed up at that housewarming in Paris than for a party I'd recently thrown at my Woodside, California, home. The festivities lasted from dusk till almost dawn.

At around 9 p.m. I looked up and noticed that my former Atari employee, Steve Jobs, was at the door. I smiled, and Steve rolled his eyes—I think he was a little taken aback at the size of the place. While I was going through a grandiose period, Steve was the same as ever: not really a grand kind of guy.

"Hey," I told him, "glad you could make it."

"If you're going to have a party in Paris, I'm going to be the last guy to miss it," he replied. "Anyway, I needed a vacation."

I asked how long he'd be in town, and he said a few days.

"Let's have breakfast tomorrow, then," I offered, and he agreed.

As we continued to talk, I noticed that Steve's appearance had changed since he'd worked for me at Atari—in fact, each time I'd seen him since, he'd been better dressed, more adult looking. This night he was wearing his usual Levi's 501s but, remarkably, they were clean. And although his hair was still long, he'd actually washed it before showing up.

On top of that, Steve's manners were impeccable. It seemed as if he had civilized himself. Although he had been a terrific employee at Atari, no one could say he'd been terrific with people.

At this time his new company, Apple, was already quite successful, probably doing a little less than one hundred million dollars in sales—but nothing close to what Atari or Chuck E. Cheese's was earning. In 1980, Atari was bringing in around two billion dollars in revenue and Chuck E. Cheese's some five hundred million. I still didn't feel too bad that I had turned down a one-third ownership of Apple—although I was beginning to think it might turn out to be a mistake.

I was quite proud of Steve and felt a part of his success. Atari had helped him a great deal. For example, we'd given him computer parts and let him buy microprocessors at cost—in fact, almost all the early Apple parts came from Atari, without markup. The Apple modulator, a very tricky device that allowed the Apple II to connect to a television set, was based on our off-the-shelf design.

Steve and I spent the next day together. Acting as tour guide, I showed him my favorite places, including the café Les Deux Magots, where we sat for hours and talked about creativity. I told him that Paris brought out my best ideas: "There's something about this place that's excellent for thinking big thoughts." He agreed.

We then walked around the city for hours. I continued to point out my favorite places to visit, but Steve was most interested in two things: all the creativity he sensed, and the architecture.

"It's really neat to see so much creativity," he said. "So many people doing their thing and evidently making a living at it." He talked at length about the historic Parisian writers' and artists' salons. And then he added, "The computer is going to allow even more people to be creative."

Around this time, Steve had started to regard the computer as the equivalent of a bicycle for our minds. "If you look at the fastest animals, human beings aren't among them," he said, "unless you give them a bicycle, and then they can win the race."

The city's architecture fascinated him as well: He saw a simplicity and uniformity of design in the buildings—so many of them seven or eight stories tall and made of similar yellow stone, exuding an elegance and consistency that instilled a sense of harmony in the brain.

I was having a hard time thinking of Paris as having such simplicity and uniformity. But Steve's point was that you could parachute anywhere into the city and realize you were nowhere but Paris. "There aren't many cities where you can do that," he pointed out. "The architecture here creates a unique signature for the entire city."

That Parisian simplicity was something he wanted Apple to emulate.

After walking and talking all day, we again sat down at a café. I ordered a cappuccino and Steve ordered tea—he was a big tea drinker. I asked him how he thought Apple was doing, and he confessed he was worried the company wasn't being innovative enough. He wasn't happy with the current products, and he wondered what the next wave of computers was going to look like, and what new innovations would come along.

"How in the world do you figure out what the next big thing is?" he asked.

I replied, "You have to be aware of everything that's going on, and be open to adapting to it. In your case, what you want to do is discover what people like about the latest developments on the mainframes, where money is no object, and then figure out a way to make these things cheap and accessible."

"Well, that's what I'm doing," he responded, telling me that this was what the then-state-of-the-art Apple II was about: "making computer power accessible." I agreed. In many ways the Apple II was more powerful than an IBM mainframe from ten years earlier.

Steve and I talked about many other computer-related subjects, from processing speed to 16-bit architecture. Most of all, we tried to predict the future. Steve was totally preoccupied with the evolution of Apple products. "How do we keep ahead of the game?" he wanted to know.

"You've got to figure out how to put yourself in the future and ask, 'What do I want my computer to do?'" I said. "'What are the things that it can't do now that I really want it to do?'"

He nodded. "We're trying to do that. It's difficult, though. It's hard to find people who can think that way."

He was also convinced that his competitors were constantly copying Apple: "There are parasites all over the computer world ready to take whatever we come up with," he fumed.

I told him that imitation was a form of compliment, which he understood.

Then he sighed. "Everybody expects me to come up with all the ideas. That's not how you build a strong company."

He went on to explain that he needed to generate more creativity within the company. We both recognized that innovation was the key to the future, and innovation was going to have to come from the brilliance of all the people at Apple—not just the person on top.

What I realized then was that the original Steve Jobs believed he had to find his own next Steve Jobs.

We spent the rest of the day talking about issues related to creativity. At the time, I came up with dozens of suggestions for Steve, many of which he wrote down. I kept thinking that I should write them down too, and publish them in a book.

Now, three decades later, I have.

* * *

One of the ideas Steve and I addressed was the concept of rules. Neither of us felt that creativity could thrive in the presence of strict ones. Thus, the book you're reading contains no rules. Instead, it has pongs.

I use pongs because it gives me a chance to reintroduce a word that originated with the video game I created with my friend, engineer Al Alcorn, in 1972.

A pong is a piece of advice (and in the case of this particular book, advice designed to help enhance creativity). It applies only where the advice is helpful or needed, unlike a rule, which thinks of itself as applicable to every situation.

That is probably why most rules don't work. Situations vary. Flexibility is always necessary. If you try to apply the same rules to every person or circumstance, you will find you've planted a field that is sterile and homogenous. In that environment creativity will wither and die. The constant application of inflexible rules stifles the imagination.

For example, when I was the CEO of Atari—and still young enough to try to establish rules—we had a rule stating that employees could not bring their dogs into the office. After all, the workplace was chaotic enough without adding canines to it. But then we ran into a brilliant engineer who loved his dog so much he absolutely insisted on being able to bring her to work—otherwise, the engineer said, he would simply turn down our offer and find work elsewhere. We would have not been able to hire this man and add his exceptional creative talents to our mix if we hadn't decided to relax the no-dog rule.

However, making an exception didn't resolve the issue. When other people saw this man bring in his dog, they wanted to bring in theirs as well. We then had to find an inventive solution to keep the workplace from turning into a kennel, so we came up with a Solomonic decision: Other people weren't permitted to bring their dogs to work *every* day, but they could on special occasions. Everyone agreed. Problem solved.

(We ended up liking the engineer's particular dog so much we decided to "hire" her by giving her a badge and an employee number. We then announced that other special dogs could also apply and be hired for a job if they were qualified. Another rule broken. Some day I will write a book on how to hire creative dogs.)

The truth is, there are no rules that apply to everyone uniformly—and that rule is the one exception to the rule that there are no rules.

So, then: following are fifty-one pongs to help you and your company create an environment in which creativity can flourish.

Why creativity?

Because as Steve and I discussed that day in Paris, without creativity your company will not succeed. That concept may not sound surprising, but what *is* surprising is how few companies realize it, or actually do anything about it. Creativity is every company's first driver. It's where everything starts, where energy and forward motion originate. Without that first charge of creativity, nothing else can take place.

Of course, some businesses are more aware of this requirement than others. Hollywood, the gaming industry, the publishing business—they all must stay on top of their markets. *Pong* was a terrific video game, but after you'd played it ten thousand times, you wanted to move on to another game. *Star Wars* was a wonderful movie, but once you'd seen it (perhaps ten thousand times), you were ready for a new and different cinematic experience. In the entertainment field, the creatives are not just important members of the team—they're critical.

But almost all other types of companies are equally creative dependent. They just don't know it.

The reason for this dependence is competition. Just about every company faces some form of competition. All of your competitors are trying to improve the product, the service, the concept; they're creating new markets, refining processes to cut costs, and making their businesses more efficient. That's what good businesses do. The ones that don't inevitably wake up one day and find they have been outgunned, outclassed, and are out of business. As management guru Peter Drucker said, "The only source of sustained competitive advantage is the ability to learn faster than your competitors."

Fast is important. The era when companies slowly evolved, when they studied their place in the business landscape over many years and changed slowly, is over. Today, companies have to radically revolutionize themselves every few years just to stay relevant.

That's because technology and the Internet have transformed the business landscape forever. And the pace of change accelerates every year. Think about what's happened over the last few decades. A letter that once took three days to deliver to a mailbox now takes three seconds to arrive in an inbox. A transatlantic order that once required a costly telex machine to transmit can now be completed at the push of a button on a smartphone. A face-to-face meeting that once meant weeks of planning and miles of travel can now be conducted instantaneously via Skype. Once, if you wanted to test-market an idea, it took three weeks or longer to gather and crunch the data. Now you can get it coded and tested out on the Internet in one afternoon.

Ideas happen faster, knowledge moves faster, competitors react faster. So it doesn't matter what you do or your company does. The odds are overwhelming that you are going to have to change, and change again, and then again. You may be happy selling soap, and consumers will always need it, but the kind of soap they want will alter, as will its container, its smell, and its role in their lives.

As the world changes, you need to make sure your entire company shapes your product to suit the shape of the new society—and that new society is coming, whether you want it to or not. The key to survival in this new world is creativity.

So every company needs to make sure it is constantly pushing the envelope, because it takes time to move a new process or project into the marketplace efficiently. Few companies can innovate on a dime. The ability to move quickly must always be present. That ability exists only where creativity thrives.

Furthermore, this openness to creativity must be present at all levels of your company. Creativity doesn't reside in one person, or even a few people. It must be planted throughout the entire company, or it won't bloom anywhere.

The person who identifies a problem is part of the creativity chain. The person who thinks of a solution is also part of the chain. The person who executes the solution is yet another part of the chain, as is the person who then moves that solution into the mainstream, through marketing or production.

All these DNA-like links must be in place for the fruits of creativity to flourish. Each of the people involved is creative in his or her own way. Everyone must do his or her part or nothing gets done, and the ideas remain stillborn.

For example, I remember one beautiful Sunday morning

in May when Steve Jobs visited my house in Woodside. Steve brewed some tea with one of the odd Indian tea bags he carried and I drank my usual espresso macchiato. We then strolled up to the redwood grove behind my house and sat on our favorite rocks as he talked about getting too much of the credit for Apple's creativity. I told him that the feeling was natural and that it had been happening to me for as long as I had been running Atari. People always gave me the credit for inventing *Pong* when, in fact, Al Alcorn had engineered many of the innovations that made it such a great game.

What I actually did was to see a great market for the game, and then proceed with the plan I'd created. Similarly, I told Steve, it might have been Apple co-founder Steve Wozniak's computer design that was groundbreaking, but it was he, Steve Jobs, who had seen its full potential. "You both were responsible for getting it onto the market—who gets credit for the creativity is irrelevant."

Creativity must flow freely and liberally throughout the entire company, and will only succeed if a succession of many people is in place to guide it along, from the Steve Jobses at the top of the chain all the way down to the potential Steve Jobses at the bottom who will, someday, be the architects of your future. Without these people guiding your imagination and your company, there is no future.

Reinvention

Many successful companies went out of business because they were not able to change with the times. Other companies, however, have been able to completely reinvent themselves—and prosper as a result. For example, jeweler Tiffany & Co. started out as a stationery store. Telephone maker Nokia was once a paper mill. Conglomerate-holding company Berkshire Hathaway began as a textile manufacturer. Kutol Products was a Cincinnati-based soap company that manufactured wallpaper cleaner as well; the cleaner business began to fade, so the company turned the product into a cute little toy, which they eventually called Play-Doh (which has sold more than two billion cans). Then there's the 3M company (which began life as the Minnesota Mining and Manufacturing Company, selling the mineral corundum), which has designed and brought more than 55,000 different products to market. The company basically reinvents itself every decade or so: About one-third of the company's annual revenue is derived from products that are less than five years old.

FINDING AND HIRING THE NEXT STEVE JOBS

SECTION ONE

MAKE YOUR WORKPLACE AN ADVERTISEMENT FOR YOUR COMPANY

ADOPT FLEXIBLE PONGS ADVERTISE CREATIVELY HIRE FOR PASSION AND INTENSITY IGNORE CREDENTIALS LOOK FOR HOBBIES USE EMPLOYEES AS RESOURCES AVOID THE CLONES HIRE THE OBNOXIOUS HIRE THE CRAZY FIND THE BULLIED LOOK FOR THE LURKERS ASK ABOUT BOOKS SAIL A BOAT HIRE UNDER YOUR NOSE COMB THROUGH TWEETS VISIT CREATIVE COMMUNITIES BEWARE OF POSEURS ASK ODD QUESTIONS CONDUCT DEEP INTERVIEWS CELEBRATE INSTITUTE A DEGREE OF ANARCHY PROMOTE PRANKSTERISM SKUNK IT UP FOSTER FAIRNESS ISOLATE CHAMPION THE BAD IDEAS CELEBRATE FAILURE REQUIRE RISK REWARD TURKEYS MENTOR TREAT EMPLOYEES AS ADULTS CREATE A CREATIVE CHAIN CREATE A CREATIVE SPACE DESIGNATE A DEMO DAY ENCOURAGE ADHD PRELOAD LEARN TO TALK CREATIVE THINK TOYS NEUTRALIZE THE NAYSAYERS WRITE DOWN OBJECTIONS TAKE CREATIVES TO CREATIVE PLACES MAKE SOMETHING FOR THE RICH CHANGE EVERY DAY, EVERY HOUR THROW THE DICE DUCK PROCESSES TAKE A RANDOM WALK THROUGH WIKIPEDIA DON'T COUNT ON ACCOUNTING INVENT HAPHAZARD HOLIDAYS MIX IT UP GO TO SLEEP

1

Atari didn't find Steve Jobs. We made it easy for him to find us. A good company is a 24/7 advertisement for itself.

Back in the mid-1970s, Atari wasn't your average large company. Our quirky environment allowed creative people to thrive, and these people acted as a living, breathing billboard for the company. They talked a great deal about Atari—about what it did, about its products, but mostly about how much fun it was to work there.

For example, at a time when most businesses' lobbies were as warm and friendly as a mortuary's, our main lobby area was basically an electronic games arcade. We were making our living from arcade games. Why not make them available for everyone to play? Everyone did, and they loved it, and told their friends.

Actually, the entire lobby was goofy, decorated with redwoods and ferns that made it seem as though you were entering an exotic jungle, not a corporation. That, too, helped create our image as a place where imagination flourished.

(I don't remember who was responsible for the Amazon-like entry, but that's not a memory lapse. At Atari, top management empowered employees to take interesting actions without permission. So while I'm sure someone very talented created the lobby environment, I probably never knew who it was.)

Everything Atari did reflected an environment that was fun and inviting, but perhaps nothing spoke more clearly of that than our Friday beer busts on the back loading dock. The parties consisted of a few kegs, some pizza, and some music, so they cost almost nothing. (Occasionally we had to pay a live band up to fifty dollars.) These blasts were a reward for hitting the sales quota (which we always did) and a great way to bring everyone together—and that really meant everyone, from the most senior executives to whoever had just been hired for the production line. We mingled, drank beer, and had an altogether awesome time (see pong 21).

These parties became synonymous with the company culture. Soon we were inviting anyone whom we were considering hiring. This practice gave us a chance to see the person in a relaxed environment and, more importantly, it gave him or her a chance to see how much fun the company was.

Today, if you want to know more about a company, you visit that company's website. You are typically directed to a tab that takes you to a page inviting you to learn more about the firm and its employment opportunities. It's invariably the most boring page you have seen in your entire life. One look and you know that working for that company is going to be dreadful.

I can think of several companies right now that actually aren't such bad places, but their sites are so dull that no one could possibly be enticed to apply for a job there. If you want ordinary employees, then you promote your company as an ordinary workplace. If you want creative employees, then you demonstrate creativity. Yet few companies are willing to do that. Most don't want to take chances, and that stagnancy shows on their websites.

Your company image is either a recruitment ad or a piece of negative PR. Consider its name. When the Steves—Jobs and Wozniak—were trying to think of a name for their computer company, Jobs was working part time at a communal farm in Oregon and eating a fruitarian diet. He thought "Apple" sounded peaceful and user friendly, traits that reflected the philosophy behind their computers. But when the two men announced their selection, the name was widely mocked. A company name should have the gravitas of a Hewlett-Packard or an International Business Machines, people said. Apple? Silly. But in the long run, the Apple name has been enormously helpful in creating and sustaining its image as a creative company.

The sense of fun embodied in that name has been implanted throughout the company over its entire history. And Apple's image has been carefully nurtured as one of a hip company making hip products. This image soon became a self-fulfilling prophecy.

When the concept of company-as-advertisement is done correctly, it allows you to sustain a creative ecosystem to which creative people are attracted, both as customers and as employees.

Another way to show the world your company is creative and interesting is to adopt odd job titles. Who needs another universe of executive vice presidents and assistant general managers? At TOMS, the California-based company that gives away a pair of shoes to a child in need for every pair sold, there are no traditional titles. Founder Blake Mycoskie is the Chief Shoe Giver. Other titles include Shoe Glue, Straight Shoeter, Shoe Dude, and Shoe-per-Woman.

Another company that's its own self-advertisement also happens to sell shoes. It's Zappos, the online retailer. At company headquarters, there's a sign posted near the human resources department featuring the image of a man with a mullet haircut, captioned "Business in the front… Party in the back." Visitors to the careers page on the company's website find an eccentric "Zappos Family Music Video" in which employees hula-hoop, do back flips, and wear hotdog and ketchup-bottle costumes. The page also highlights NERF-gun wars along with karaoke and Oreo-eating contests as regular staples of the company's culture. Zappos' reputation as one of the most enjoyable companies to work at means that only one percent of applicants actually get hired.

Much of life is about creating an appropriate ecosystem. Every individual has one. I have one. You have one. What are your values—what do you stand for? What are your passions? What are your quirks? Most important, in what type of atmosphere do you thrive? All of these traits will define your individual ecosystem. Similarly, companies have ecosystems that reflect the choices made by the CEO, the executives and, in general, their first dozen or so employees. Your company's ecosystem also becomes its living, breathing advertisement.

Those first dozen people in a company form the seed kernels around which the corporate culture will mold itself. A dozen individuals are sufficient for a dynamic to get going; beyond that number, everyone else will probably conform to the ethos they've established. In several of my companies there have been one or two outliers, though, and I've found that if you don't take care of them, change them, or get rid of them early on, they can form a toxic pod that sprouts an atrophic branch in your company.

I once tried to change an entire company's DNA. In the early 1990s, I bought a firm that made some interesting products but also had a terrible corporate culture. The place had been on a five-year decline and most of the innovative people had left. I should have fired 90 percent of the staff but I didn't; I thought I could turn the company around. I was wrong. The employees could not seem to get out of their own way. For every proposed step forward, five people resisted the change. The corporate ecosystem was contaminated. This was one of my worst failures.

Secrets

People like secrets. Creative people *really* like secrets. They're fun, imaginative, and they add a sense of excitement to any corporate culture. Apple has always fostered this culture of secrets. As an Apple employee, you may know that your friends outside Apple are dying to learn about the company's next product—even if you yourself actually know nothing. You don't even have to be in on the secret to have fun—others assume you are and since you can't tell anyway, you're safe.

Several other companies also do this well, such as Activision and Electronic Arts in the video-game business. They hide the features of their next gaming revolutions, and their employees love that they're not supposed to talk about it. Being let in on a secret was fun when you were in grammar school. It's still fun when you're an adult.

INTRODUCTION
MAKE YOUR WORKPLACE AN ADVERTISEMENT
FOR YOUR COMPANY **ADOPT FLEXIBLE PONGS**
ADVERTISE CREATIVELY HIRE FOR PASSION
AND INTENSITY IGNORE CREDENTIALS LOOK
FOR HOBBIES USE EMPLOYEES AS RESOURCES
AVOID THE CLONES HIRE THE OBNOXIOUS HIRE
THE CRAZY FIND THE BULLIED LOOK FOR THE
LURKERS ASK ABOUT BOOKS SAIL A BOAT HIRE
UNDER YOUR NOSE COMB THROUGH TWEETS
VISIT CREATIVE COMMUNITIES BEWARE OF
POSEURS ASK ODD QUESTIONS CONDUCT DEEP
INTERVIEWS CELEBRATE INSTITUTE A DEGREE OF
ANARCHY PROMOTE PRANKSTERISM SKUNK IT
UP FOSTER FAIRNESS ISOLATE CHAMPION THE
BAD IDEAS CELEBRATE FAILURE REQUIRE RISK
REWARD TURKEYS MENTOR TREAT EMPLOYEES
AS ADULTS CREATE A CREATIVE CHAIN CREATE
A CREATIVE SPACE DESIGNATE A DEMO DAY
ENCOURAGE ADHD PRELOAD LEARN TO
TALK CREATIVE THINK TOYS NEUTRALIZE THE
NAYSAYERS WRITE DOWN OBJECTIONS TAKE
CREATIVESTOCREATIVEPLACESMAKESOMETHING
FOR THE RICH CHANGE EVERY DAY, EVERY
HOUR THROW THE DICE DUCK PROCESSES
TAKE A RANDOM WALK THROUGH WIKIPEDIA
DON'T COUNT ON ACCOUNTING INVENT
HAPHAZARD HOLIDAYS MIX IT UP GO TO SLEEP
CONCLUSION

2

Managing creatives is like herding cats. You can try and try, but in the end you'll fail. So instead of establishing dispiriting rules at your company, create an organization known for its flexible and original pongs. The creatives will come crawling out of their cozy lairs, looking for a place to settle down. You can't ever really control them, but if you offer them a good work environment and stretchy guidelines, you can elicit excellent performances from them—making you, them, your company, and your stakeholders all very happy.

The alternative is establishing an environment so rigid and standardized that the only people who like it are those who are already rigid and standardized.

For example, when Steve Jobs first came to work at Atari, he wanted to be able to sleep overnight at the office. We always had a guard on the premises, but there were alarms as well. If people were sleeping under desks and moving about at 3 a.m., the alarms would have been blaring nonstop. So there were rules: No overnight sleeping at the office.

But Steve was insistent. He had to sleep at work. Otherwise, he would quit. His friend Steve Wozniak felt the same way. Our chief of security, however, was equally insistent that we should not allow it. But in the end we decided to permit overnight sleeping and rely on just the guards rather than the alarms for security, because we wanted to create a comfortable environment for the Steves.

Soon the Steves brought in futons and stored them under their desks so they could work until 3 a.m. and then catch five or six hours of sleep. There wasn't any place to shower or bathe.

Once we allowed sleepovers, we found that several other employees with long commutes decided they'd prefer to stay over at the company as well. So we went the extra mile and added showers to one of the restrooms. Some of the staff actually did like bathing. And we liked them for that.

Our engineers loved their new freedom to stay up and work as long as they liked. Once, just before a particularly intense trade show, we had more than twenty of them working late and sleeping at the company. The productivity was out of this world.

My growing awareness of rule flexibility was put to an extreme test when, at another of my companies, I found that a spare room behind the furnace had been taken over by two engineers who had decided to live there full time. They had moved in quite a few of their belongings, had bought a hot plate, and were saving a great deal of money by not paying rent or commuting costs. I decided to let them be. In some ways, this was the start of the live/work lofts that are now the staple of startups. Several Silicon Valley companies now have bunkrooms that allow employees to spend as much time at work as necessary.

(It's been said that many people in high tech cannot balance their personal and work lives. Here's another way to look at it: Their jobs are so interesting that it's difficult to figure out what is work and what is play. Creative projects produce this kind of excitement.)

The point is that when you're trying to make your company more creative, you want to relax the rigid rules and give your creatives room to stretch and grow. Create a company known for this kind of freedom, and creatives will come looking for you.

Note: Pongs rule, and rules generally have no place, but there are occasional situations in which rules must stay rules. For instance, at Atari, one of the workers in the assembly department wanted to bring his gun into work with him. To be fair, we did consider the idea instead of immediately saying no. But as the gun owner's manager pointed out, it's much harder to discipline an employee who has a gun on his hip than one who doesn't. The no-firearms policy remained in effect. So even the rule about no rules can't be taken as a rule.

INTRODUCTION
MAKE YOUR WORKPLACE AN ADVERTISEMENT
FOR YOUR COMPANY ADOPT FLEXIBLE PONGS
ADVERTISE CREATIVELY HIRE FOR PASSION
AND INTENSITY IGNORE CREDENTIALS LOOK
FOR HOBBIES USE EMPLOYEES AS RESOURCES
AVOID THE CLONES HIRE THE OBNOXIOUS HIRE
THE CRAZY FIND THE BULLIED LOOK FOR THE
LURKERS ASK ABOUT BOOKS SAIL A BOAT HIRE
UNDER YOUR NOSE COMB THROUGH TWEETS
VISIT CREATIVE COMMUNITIES BEWARE OF
POSEURS ASK ODD QUESTIONS CONDUCT DEEP
INTERVIEWS CELEBRATE INSTITUTE A DEGREE OF
ANARCHY PROMOTE PRANKSTERISM SKUNK IT
UP FOSTER FAIRNESS ISOLATE CHAMPION THE
BAD IDEAS CELEBRATE FAILURE REQUIRE RISK
REWARD TURKEYS MENTOR TREAT EMPLOYEES
AS ADULTS CREATE A CREATIVE CHAIN CREATE
A CREATIVE SPACE DESIGNATE A DEMO DAY
ENCOURAGE ADHD PRELOAD LEARN TO
TALK CREATIVE THINK TOYS NEUTRALIZE THE
NAYSAYERS WRITE DOWN OBJECTIONS TAKE
CREATIVESTOCREATIVEPLACESMAKESOMETHING
FOR THE RICH CHANGE EVERY DAY, EVERY
HOUR THROW THE DICE DUCK PROCESSES
TAKE A RANDOM WALK THROUGH WIKIPEDIA
DON'T COUNT ON ACCOUNTING INVENT
HAPHAZARD HOLIDAYS MIX IT UP GO TO SLEEP
CONCLUSION

3

There was a time when job openings were straightforwardly announced: You placed an ad in the newspaper and hoped for the best. But whatever words they used, most companies' ads effectively said, "Wanted: middle manager for boring job. Low pay. Don't bother."

At Atari, we decided to go a different route, using the advertising tag line "Play games, make money." It did very well for us, as did these lines: "Make games that make money; keep some of it," "Confusing work with play every day," and "Work harder at having fun than ever before."

We also had a program that we called a sabbatical: After each seven years of service, employees were awarded the whole summer off. I felt everybody needed time to reset. So we advertised it this way: "Frolic a whole summer every seven years, full pay."

That also worked very nicely for us.

An advertisement for help is, in effect, an advertisement for your entire company. You can't just go out with an ad that states the facts. You need to create a unique look, feel, and tag line. So at Chuck E. Cheese's, we ran funny ads: "Work for a rat, earn lots of cheese," "Make dough, make fun, have fun, earn dough," "Build rats that talk."

Fact: Funny people tend to be more creative than unfunny people.

Today there are plenty of places to advertise besides a newspaper. You can choose anywhere from Craigslist to Google to Monster.com. But today's help-wanted environment is so crowded that your ad is not likely to stand out unless you make a concerted (and creative) effort. And unfortunately, most companies are still not being very creative.

I'm getting ready to hire for my next venture, and when I do we'll create a YouTube ad—an odd, unusual one at that. Any company looking for creatives should consider making a series of strange or interesting videos that have the possibility of going viral. The videos might be really bad, or even very amateurish. But they will get attention, and let people know your company has a sense of humor (as well as some very bad actors).

And I'll want the venture's website and jobs page to be lively, fun, and enticing. Maybe we'll show the most recent hire, and he's a Labrador retriever. Perhaps we'll even turn the application process into a game, a spoof on most companies' brain-dead approach to hiring. Or we'll get current employees to create a video, something funny or odd that shows that the people in the company know how to have fun. Again, it doesn't have to be good. It just has to be fun. If you can get potential employees to smile, you're already on the road to finding your creatives.

Not long ago, computer game company Red 5 Studios poached talent from other companies by recording personalized messages on iPods and sending them to their top 100 prospects. In doing this the company was able to fill three major positions, spend much less than they otherwise would have for a traditional recruitment campaign, and receive a great deal of positive attention from everyone (except the companies whose employees they'd poached).

Another example: The German branch of advertising company BBDO, which was looking to recruit copywriters from a university, took a mass-media approach, with a creative twist.

Playing off the notion that young artists often scribble their first masterpiece on a napkin, the company printed its recruitment message on napkins distributed at the university's cafeteria. From two thousand napkins, they received roughly four hundred calls.

And one of my favorites: The Australian branch of the furniture company IKEA advertised for employees by including funny "career assembly instructions" with the packaging of many of their products. They claim 4,285 applications made and 280 careers assembled from the effort.

Of course, the creative people who answer such ads may also use an unorthodox approach. Someone told me a story about a young man who had recently been hired when his boss called him into his office. "When you answered our ad, you told us you had five years of experience," the boss said. "We've checked your background, and as far as we can tell, this is your first job. How do you explain that?"

The young man replied, "Well, your ad said that you wanted somebody who was very creative."

I N T R O D U C T I O N
MAKE YOUR WORKPLACE AN ADVERTISEMENT
FOR YOUR COMPANY ADOPT FLEXIBLE PONGS
ADVERTISE CREATIVELY **HIRE FOR PASSION
AND INTENSITY** IGNORE CREDENTIALS LOOK
FOR HOBBIES USE EMPLOYEES AS RESOURCES
AVOID THE CLONES HIRE THE OBNOXIOUS HIRE
THE CRAZY FIND THE BULLIED LOOK FOR THE
LURKERS ASK ABOUT BOOKS SAIL A BOAT HIRE
UNDER YOUR NOSE COMB THROUGH TWEETS
VISIT CREATIVE COMMUNITIES BEWARE OF
POSEURS ASK ODD QUESTIONS CONDUCT DEEP
INTERVIEWS CELEBRATE INSTITUTE A DEGREE OF
ANARCHY PROMOTE PRANKSTERISM SKUNK IT
UP FOSTER FAIRNESS ISOLATE CHAMPION THE
BAD IDEAS CELEBRATE FAILURE REQUIRE RISK
REWARD TURKEYS MENTOR TREAT EMPLOYEES
AS ADULTS CREATE A CREATIVE CHAIN CREATE
A CREATIVE SPACE DESIGNATE A DEMO DAY
ENCOURAGE ADHD PRELOAD LEARN TO
TALK CREATIVE THINK TOYS NEUTRALIZE THE
NAYSAYERS WRITE DOWN OBJECTIONS TAKE
CREATIVES TO CREATIVE PLACES MAKE SOMETHING
FOR THE RICH CHANGE EVERY DAY, EVERY
HOUR THROW THE DICE DUCK PROCESSES
TAKE A RANDOM WALK THROUGH WIKIPEDIA
DON'T COUNT ON ACCOUNTING INVENT
HAPHAZARD HOLIDAYS MIX IT UP GO TO SLEEP
C O N C L U S I O N

4

If there was a single characteristic that separated Steve Jobs from the mass of employees, it was his passionate enthusiasm. Steve had one speed: full blast.

This was the primary reason we hired him.

When you hire for intensity, you are bringing in people around whom you can build an entire department. For instance, I once hired a woman who showed up at our office with virtually no business experience. But her passionate nature was so obvious that, although she was only nineteen, we hired her to help us with trade shows. No matter how little time was left before the event started, this woman always managed to get every carpet vacuumed, every box unpacked, and every display set up. By the time she was twenty she was running a department. Today, she has her own company.

One of the reasons behind Atari's success was that we always looked for, and hired, such people. You can train employees in the ways of the company, but you can't train them to be passionate. In the long run, people with enthusiasm are going to contribute the most to your enterprise.

Not long ago I ran into a woman at a Mindshare, a salon in Los Angeles where professionals in fields such as movies, television, technology, and architecture gather once a month to hear speakers, network, and have a good time. This woman cornered me and extracted so much information about my current education project that I almost felt as though I was being interrogated by a government agent.

I had no idea why I was telling her so many secrets. But after hearing what I had to say, she reeled off twenty excellent marketing ideas. Finally, she asked for a job. I was so impressed with her intensity that I hired her right on the spot. One of the seed crystals of my new education company, she now oversees our web presence and is running our marketing department. She, too, has one speed: full blast.

How do you find passion? It's a little like U.S. Supreme Court Associate Justice Potter Stewart's remark about pornography—it's hard to define, but you know it when you see it. And the first place you see it is in the eyes. Steve Jobs used to look other people straight in the eye, with no waffling, totally focused and in the present. At an interview, people with passion do not look shifty. Like Steve, they look you in the eye, knowing it's their job to convince you to hire them.

And when passionate people talk at that interview, they don't ramble on about themselves or ask you a lot of questions; they gush about the company. They've done some research, and they know what they want to discuss; it's almost as if they have a script running in their heads before they come to the door. They enter prepared to talk about ideas rather than their résumé.

Conversely, one of the best ways to spot applicants without passion is to listen to how they describe their lives. The passionless tend to be blamers. Ask a targeted question about several of their previous employers, and you'll discover a great deal.

For example, "Why were you fired from your last job?"

A good answer: "My skill set wasn't appropriate for the new direction, and I couldn't learn it fast enough. It was my mistake."

A bad answer: "My boss had it out for me."

Consider another question: "Why did you get bad grades?"

A good answer: "I partied too much. If I knew how important it was going to be to get good grades, I wouldn't have done that."

A bad answer: "My parents wouldn't pay for my education, so I had to work two jobs while I was in college."

Some of these excuses may be true—but they're not the way passionate people present themselves. The passionate talk about what they *want* and can *do*; they don't tick off reasons why they haven't done it yet.

Anytime you're meeting with prospective employees, whether at a cocktail party or a formal interview, ask them to talk about their passions. For those who don't have any, the resulting silence can be painful. For those who do, it's like watching a dam break. You get a tsunami of information about something that, until this moment, you knew nothing. That doesn't matter. What is said is far less important than the way it is said. A person's passion can be about anything, from aardvarks to zydeco. It doesn't even matter if it doesn't match your mission. You can take that passion and meld it to your goal—but you can't create passion if it's not there.

A good answer, I pointed out much, "I knew how important ... ...

INTRODUCTION
MAKE YOUR WORKPLACE AN ADVERTISEMENT
FOR YOUR COMPANY ADOPT FLEXIBLE PONGS
ADVERTISE CREATIVELY HIRE FOR PASSION
AND INTENSITY **IGNORE CREDENTIALS** LOOK
FOR HOBBIES USE EMPLOYEES AS RESOURCES
AVOID THE CLONES HIRE THE OBNOXIOUS HIRE
THE CRAZY FIND THE BULLIED LOOK FOR THE
LURKERS ASK ABOUT BOOKS SAIL A BOAT HIRE
UNDER YOUR NOSE COMB THROUGH TWEETS
VISIT CREATIVE COMMUNITIES BEWARE OF
POSEURS ASK ODD QUESTIONS CONDUCT DEEP
INTERVIEWS CELEBRATE INSTITUTE A DEGREE OF
ANARCHY PROMOTE PRANKSTERISM SKUNK IT
UP FOSTER FAIRNESS ISOLATE CHAMPION THE
BAD IDEAS CELEBRATE FAILURE REQUIRE RISK
REWARD TURKEYS MENTOR TREAT EMPLOYEES
AS ADULTS CREATE A CREATIVE CHAIN CREATE
A CREATIVE SPACE DESIGNATE A DEMO DAY
ENCOURAGE ADHD PRELOAD LEARN TO
TALK CREATIVE THINK TOYS NEUTRALIZE THE
NAYSAYERS WRITE DOWN OBJECTIONS TAKE
CREATIVESTOCREATIVEPLACESMAKESOMETHING
FOR THE RICH CHANGE EVERY DAY, EVERY
HOUR THROW THE DICE DUCK PROCESSES
TAKE A RANDOM WALK THROUGH WIKIPEDIA
DON'T COUNT ON ACCOUNTING INVENT
HAPHAZARD HOLIDAYS MIX IT UP GO TO SLEEP
CONCLUSION

5

I believe we are moving away from a credentialed society to a merit-based society.

A college degree, for example, is a fairly meaningless credential. It tells you that someone has a certain amount of stick-to-itiveness and managed to get through school. It does not tell you much else. Graduating from college, in itself, is not a sign of intelligence. It could mean that someone is smart, or merely that he figured out how to pass a test and then, after collecting bushels of good grades, forgot everything he learned.

Over the years I have found that many of the best creatives did not graduate from college. Steve Jobs dropped out, as did Steve Wozniak. So did Microsoft's Bill Gates, DreamWorks Studios' David Geffen, Facebook's Mark Zuckerberg, haute couture designer Coco Chanel, cartoon producer William Hanna, and countless others.

I'm not recommending people avoid college. College can be a wonderful experience, in terms of both education and socialization. I am recommending that employers stop using a college degree as the be-all-and-end-all qualification for employment. Insisting that all job applicants have a college degree is foolish. Many creative people have a difficult time putting up with the often silly busy work involved in obtaining a degree.

Interestingly, a 2008 study reported in *The Journal of Marketing Education* suggested that most of the knowledge students gained in their respective majors was lost within two years. Students who received an A in these classes actually lost their knowledge at a faster rate than the students who got a C.

Rather than ask job candidates obvious questions about their background, their classes, their teachers—everyone can answer them, especially if this is their umpteenth interview—I like to ask a series of odd questions they couldn't possibly answer, but about which they can make some interesting guesses using a series of logical assumptions.

For instance, I have often asked potential employees how many pounds of rice are eaten in China every year. This tests their knowledge of China's population and the amount of food someone might eat in a meal. Most smart people can probably get to a number that isn't ridiculously far off. I have no idea what the correct answer is. I don't care. More important to me is the chance to observe someone's problem-solving process.

Try it: Pose questions that people really need to puzzle over. Pay attention as they do so. (See pong 19 for more about questions.)

Another test I still like to employ: Place a person in a room with access to resources, but without making them obvious. You want to see how people find answers. Today I give applicants access to the Internet, but in the pre-Internet days I would simply leave a few reference books and a telephone. I told the applicants that how they got the answer to my question wasn't as important as being able to get one. The ones who called a library or a friend were resourceful. The ones who couldn't figure out what to do and just guessed were not.

When dealing with engineers, instead of posing a question I might suddenly ask them to wire a pair of light switches at the top and bottom of a staircase. It's a simple trick, but if an engineer doesn't have the curiosity to figure out how it's done, it shows me that this person may be an engineer by training, but lacks the DNA of a true seeker of scientific knowledge.

What you are trying to discover through these unusual questions and tests is a person possessing a combination of curiosity and resourcefulness. I know of no creative who is not hyper-curious. Curious people always have a range of interests and a broad base of knowledge in many disparate fields and subjects. This trait has nothing to do with college. It has everything to do with innate intelligence.

6

One of the best ways to uncover the creative passion of potential job candidates is to ask about their hobbies, particularly ones that are difficult or complex, somewhat time consuming, or suggest a large appetite for intellectual challenge.

For instance, in my case, I was a rabid fan of ham radio, as were most geeks in the 1950s and 1960s. Ham radio was a technology for everyone—advanced but accessible—and if you could figure out how to build one, you could talk to someone in Europe for free at a time when a transatlantic phone call cost twenty dollars (a lot of money back then). There was a social benefit as well: Suddenly you could chat with, and learn from, people all over the world.

My first job was at Ampex, the video and audio company that pioneered the use of the videotape recorder, and the place where I learned the craft of video engineering. My boss, Kurt Wallace, hired me in part because he was so impressed with my ham radio hobby.

Or take Al Alcorn, the most creative engineer I've ever met. I get a lot of credit for things he invented. He was constantly working on side projects, creating little doodads he was very proud of. His passion for his hobbies, which revolved mostly around cars, was reflected in his passion for work.

I remember hiring one man who impressed me because he couldn't stop talking about his model train hobby. He had devoted most of his basement to a train set, which in California is very impressive, as most houses don't have basements—but as he explained, he wouldn't live in a house without one. His love of trains helped him eventually design our joystick; in fact, he could create any little mechanism we needed because he had what I ended up calling "finger intelligence."

One job seeker came to me with the most complicated game design I had ever seen, complete with intricate drawings and arcane rules. I thought the game itself was horrible, but this example of his hobby—creating intricate games—and the process he had gone through to create it was remarkable. We hired him.

Another applicant proposed a game for marijuana smokers: Basically, it made pretty pictures move in sync with music. Since I knew that many of my employees smoked pot, I thought it might be an interesting product. I hired him and we actually ended up making the game. It was a total failure, but at least we were keeping up with the times. (Hey, this was Northern California in the early 1970s.)

Hobbies aren't just a sign of passion and creativity. When you have a hobby, you're constantly expanding your knowledge. The employee who loved model trains, for example, studied train layouts from different eras to help him decide which type he wanted to replicate. He eventually became interested in the process by which burning coal is transformed into steam to power a train. The fine points of expanding gas might not seem like practical knowledge, but someone with this interest later turns out to be just the person who understands how to create pizza parlor characters that spring to life through pneumatics.

In fact, when I first hired many of Chuck E. Cheese's engineers, I had no idea we would eventually build singing and dancing animals. When the time came to do that, these employees were able to step up to the task because of their wildly diverse interests and hobbies.

In the business world, you'll find numerous examples of people who rely on their hobbies for productivity. Stephen Gillett, executive vice president and chief operating officer at Symantec (formerly president of Best Buy Digital and executive vice president of digital ventures at Starbucks), has publicly credited his obsession with the online role-playing game *World of Warcraft* with helping him manage his on-the-job tasks. Others have even started businesses based on their hobbies. Australian-born American entrepreneur Megan Duckett, who worked at an event-planning company, began sewing in her free time. After making the linings of decorative coffins for her employer's Halloween party, she realized she'd found a niche. Duckett quit her full-time job in 1996; by then, the money coming from her side projects had surpassed her salary. In 2011, her theatrical drapery business generated $6.2 million in sales.

What unites creative people is their passion for diverse knowledge. It is the driver. Serious hobbies are a sign of this passion. In *Where Good Ideas Come From: The Natural History of Innovation*, author Steven Johnson writes, "Legendary innovators like Franklin. . . and Darwin all possess some common intellectual qualities—a certain quickness of mind, unbounded curiosity—but they also share one other defining attribute. They have a lot of hobbies."

INTRODUCTION
MAKE YOUR WORKPLACE AN ADVERTISEMENT
FOR YOUR COMPANY ADOPT FLEXIBLE PONGS
ADVERTISE CREATIVELY HIRE FOR PASSION
AND INTENSITY IGNORE CREDENTIALS LOOK
FOR HOBBIES **USE EMPLOYEES AS RESOURCES**
AVOID THE CLONES HIRE THE OBNOXIOUS HIRE
THE CRAZY FIND THE BULLIED LOOK FOR THE
LURKERS ASK ABOUT BOOKS SAIL A BOAT HIRE
UNDER YOUR NOSE COMB THROUGH TWEETS
VISIT CREATIVE COMMUNITIES BEWARE OF
POSEURS ASK ODD QUESTIONS CONDUCT DEEP
INTERVIEWS CELEBRATE INSTITUTE A DEGREE OF
ANARCHY PROMOTE PRANKSTERISM SKUNK IT
UP FOSTER FAIRNESS ISOLATE CHAMPION THE
BAD IDEAS CELEBRATE FAILURE REQUIRE RISK
REWARD TURKEYS MENTOR TREAT EMPLOYEES
AS ADULTS CREATE A CREATIVE CHAIN CREATE
A CREATIVE SPACE DESIGNATE A DEMO DAY
ENCOURAGE ADHD PRELOAD LEARN TO
TALK CREATIVE THINK TOYS NEUTRALIZE THE
NAYSAYERS WRITE DOWN OBJECTIONS TAKE
CREATIVES TO CREATIVE PLACES MAKE SOMETHING
FOR THE RICH CHANGE EVERY DAY, EVERY
HOUR THROW THE DICE DUCK PROCESSES
TAKE A RANDOM WALK THROUGH WIKIPEDIA
DON'T COUNT ON ACCOUNTING INVENT
HAPHAZARD HOLIDAYS MIX IT UP GO TO SLEEP
CONCLUSION

7

One of the best ways to find creatives is to delegate. Too often, people hoard the authority to hire. They turn it into their personal power trip; they don't like sharing.

Don't hoard. Unless the employee search must remain confidential, if you want to find creatives, ask other creatives to help you. Your current employees are a treasure trove of possibility. Use them as resources to locate people with whom they have previously worked. After all, working with others is the best way to grasp their capabilities.

Everyone has a short list of the cool people they'd love to work with again, as well as those they want nothing to do with, ever. Get those lists out of people.

This form of hiring has slowly become part of Silicon Valley DNA. I did this myself, unmercifully, at Atari. I picked Ampex dry. Three of my best hires—Al Alcorn, Steve Bristow, and Steve Mayer—came from Ampex, as did about twenty others. I even hired away Ampex's plant nurse, who everyone had told me was exceptional. This was long before we even needed a plant nurse. I just wanted such an exceptional person working for us.

Once Apple was formed, Steve Wozniak poached from his old firm, Hewlett-Packard, and Steve Jobs poached from Atari as unmercifully as I'd poached from Ampex. I lost some really good people to Steve. The one guy they didn't get was Ron Wayne, a brilliant mechanical engineer who was asked to be a partner at Apple. He turned them down. Ron had already worked at a startup and had been on the hook for some liabilities. He was loath to do it again. If he had taken the job and stayed, today his stake would be worth about twenty billion dollars.

AVOID THE CLONES.

INTRODUCTION
MAKE YOUR WORKPLACE AN ADVERTISEMENT
FOR YOUR COMPANY ADOPT FLEXIBLE PONGS
ADVERTISE CREATIVELY HIRE FOR PASSION
AND INTENSITY IGNORE CREDENTIALS LOOK
FOR HOBBIES USE EMPLOYEES AS RESOURCES
AVOID THE CLONES HIRE THE OBNOXIOUS HIRE
THE CRAZY FIND THE BULLIED LOOK FOR THE
LURKERS ASK ABOUT BOOKS SAIL A BOAT HIRE
UNDER YOUR NOSE COMB THROUGH TWEETS
VISIT CREATIVE COMMUNITIES BEWARE OF
POSEURS ASK ODD QUESTIONS CONDUCT DEEP
INTERVIEWS CELEBRATE INSTITUTE A DEGREE OF
ANARCHY PROMOTE PRANKSTERISM SKUNK IT
UP FOSTER FAIRNESS ISOLATE CHAMPION THE
BAD IDEAS CELEBRATE FAILURE REQUIRE RISK
REWARD TURKEYS MENTOR TREAT EMPLOYEES
AS ADULTS CREATE A CREATIVE CHAIN CREATE
A CREATIVE SPACE DESIGNATE A DEMO DAY
ENCOURAGE ADHD PRELOAD LEARN TO
TALK CREATIVE THINK TOYS NEUTRALIZE THE
NAYSAYERS WRITE DOWN OBJECTIONS TAKE
CREATIVESTOCREATIVEPLACESMAKESOMETHING
FOR THE RICH CHANGE EVERY DAY, EVERY
HOUR THROW THE DICE DUCK PROCESSES
TAKE A RANDOM WALK THROUGH WIKIPEDIA
DON'T COUNT ON ACCOUNTING INVENT
HAPHAZARD HOLIDAYS MIX IT UP GO TO SLEEP
CONCLUSION

8

___

Most human resources departments will tell you they want to hire a diverse range of employees. This is a good thing. But there's another important kind of diversity that these departments don't believe in: creative diversity. HR departments have a tendency to hire the same people over and over, despite apparent differences in ethnicity or gender. These are people who, regardless of race, sexual orientation, or religion, attend the same schools, believe in the same ethos, and dress the same way.

Unfortunately, most companies seek homogeneity. But homogeneity does not breed creativity. You don't want a homogenous company where everyone is interchangeable. You want a company that is spiky. Spiky balls have great singularities; in spiky companies, these singularities are the exceptional people.

Corporate culture, however, tries to grind down the spikes; most companies want a smooth, round ball. And to make that smooth, round ball, they get rid of the unconventional thinkers who could make their company successful.

If you have a human resources department, ask the people who work there how many of the company's engineers dropped out of school, how many of its passionate marketers have arm-long tattoos, and how many of its copywriters wear strange outfits. (Don't be surprised if the answer is zero.) If you happen to be the boss, tell your people that instead of hiring immaculately dressed college graduates, this month you want them to fulfill a high-school dropout quota. Without standard credentials to rely on, they'll need to find interesting ways to discover which dropouts are really exceptional applicants. That's hard work. And it can pay off handsomely.

Hiring a creative is about embracing risk, not mitigating it. So if you're starting a company, perhaps your first task is to find creatives who can hire other creatives.

Cherish the pink-haired

Eclecticism is highly undervalued in today's job market. Don't let your company dismiss people who dress differently, dye their hair pink, or wear strange jewelry. Minor insanity in the clothing department is a benefit. Every company needs physical and intellectual diversity. As discussed, such people tend to be creative.

But also consider that if you are trying to sell your product or service to customers who have pink hair or odd tattoos, yet don't employ any such people, you'll have no idea how to reach them.

Some of the best people I ever hired might have been considered somewhat freakish. For instance, the man who created the chip for *Pong*, Harold Lee, was enormous, drove a great big, tricked-out Harley, and had a huge greying beard and long straggly hair that I don't think he ever washed. Harold was a brilliant chip designer. I am sure that he would have had one hell of a time getting a job at IBM.

9

A common truism in business today is that pleasant employees are good employees. However, unpleasant employees can be even better ones.

Unbridled arrogance is obnoxious. Yet in some cases people's arrogance is well-founded because they are, indeed, the smartest ones in the room and therefore accurate about their perceived value to your company. Is it obnoxious for them to actually *tell* you this? Yes. But when you have a problem that needs a brain that can crack walnuts, you want them to get on it.

Having arrogant people around sounds like a morale dampener, but it doesn't have to be. It can even make the office more fun. You become accustomed to saying, "Give that problem to George," and then rolling your eyes. George's obnoxious personality becomes a shared joke. And George doesn't care if people don't like him; he's spent his entire life knowing that. In fact, some of the Arrogant Georges I know consider their unpopularity a badge of honor.

However, you don't want too many Arrogant Georges in your company. If everyone is the smartest person in the room, then the word "smartest" doesn't make sense anymore. Luckily, there are only a few really significantly smart and arrogant people out there, and you definitely want to hire them.

When you do, you can warn the other employees: "George is showing up on Monday. None of you are going to like him. You don't have to. He's brilliant, though, and he'll make us a better company. Don't bother asking him to lunch."

George probably doesn't want to go to lunch with any of your employees anyway, or to be taken out for a drink after his first day. He'll even roll his eyes when you talk to him about your interests, because his, he knows, are so much more interesting.

Embrace the Georges of the world. They will seek out your company if they know that it offers a refuge for them. Steve Jobs understood that Atari was the kind of place that would allow him to flourish, no matter how arrogant he seemed. Perhaps everyone has creative potential, but only the arrogant are self-confident enough to press their creative ideas on others. Steve believed he was always right, and was willing to push harder and longer than other people who might have had equally good ideas but who caved under pressure.

INTRODUCTION MAKE YOUR WORKPLACE AN ADVERTISEMENT FOR YOUR COMPANY ADOPT FLEXIBLE PONGS ADVERTISE CREATIVELY HIRE FOR PASSION AND INTENSITY IGNORE CREDENTIALS LOOK FOR HOBBIES USE EMPLOYEES AS RESOURCES AVOID THE CLONES HIRE THE OBNOXIOUS **HIRE THE CRAZY** FIND THE BULLIED LOOK FOR THE LURKERS ASK ABOUT BOOKS SAIL A BOAT HIRE UNDER YOUR NOSE COMB THROUGH TWEETS VISIT CREATIVE COMMUNITIES BEWARE OF POSEURS ASK ODD QUESTIONS CONDUCT DEEP INTERVIEWS CELEBRATE INSTITUTE A DEGREE OF ANARCHY PROMOTE PRANKSTERISM SKUNK IT UP FOSTER FAIRNESS ISOLATE CHAMPION THE BAD IDEAS CELEBRATE FAILURE REQUIRE RISK REWARD TURKEYS MENTOR TREAT EMPLOYEES AS ADULTS CREATE A CREATIVE CHAIN CREATE A CREATIVE SPACE DESIGNATE A DEMO DAY ENCOURAGE ADHD PRELOAD LEARN TO TALK CREATIVE THINK TOYS NEUTRALIZE THE NAYSAYERS WRITE DOWN OBJECTIONS TAKE CREATIVES TO CREATIVE PLACES MAKE SOMETHING FOR THE RICH CHANGE EVERY DAY, EVERY HOUR THROW THE DICE DUCK PROCESSES TAKE A RANDOM WALK THROUGH WIKIPEDIA DON'T COUNT ON ACCOUNTING INVENT HAPHAZARD HOLIDAYS MIX IT UP GO TO SLEEP CONCLUSION

10

There's a fine line between creativity and insanity. I don't mean clinical insanity—there's nothing good about that. But there's a kind of functional craziness that should inhabit your creative offices, the kind that emanates from employees who are always coming up with wacky ideas, insane-sounding concepts, and off-the-wall notions.

The problem most companies have is that the crazier the ideas their creatives present, the less likely they are to endorse and promote them. Yet, when first announced, some of the best ideas that have rocked the world were greeted with cries of "That's totally crazy!"

Frankly, most of my life people have told me I was crazy. Everyone thought my idea to found Atari was nuts. My associates at Ampex took me aside to tell me that the idea of playing games on a video screen was truly ridiculous—at the time, the only images on a video screen that anyone had ever seen were those on television. Even the idea of creating an image locally was considered nuts—I remember one very smart person asking me how the television station knew when someone turned the knob controller on *Pong*. And of course, the concept of talking animals inhabiting a giant pizza parlor was also thought to be a harebrained idea. Even now, when I use those words to explain Chuck E. Cheese's, people laugh.

Not that all my crazy ideas have worked out, of course—sometimes crazy has to come at the right time. In the 1980s, when I was working on my idea for a domestic robot companion (see pong 29), people thought the idea of little robots running around your house was absurd. As it turned out, the technology wasn't quite ready. But today I still cannot, in my wildest imagination, believe we will not someday have personal robots in our homes. To me, it's crazy to postulate a future without them. Yet the number of times I have seen people's eyes glaze over when I wax eloquent on the subject is remarkable.

Then again, when I talk about robotic cars with auto-drive, people also look at me as though I'm nuts—and yet these cars are probably only about five years away. Between the work done by Google, BMW, and several Japanese companies, the technology is there. As soon as the costs come within reason, it's going to happen.

People also said, "Crazy!" when hearing about things like the telephone—why would you want to talk to someone you can't even see when you can just walk just down the street and see her? The airplane? Crazy! If people were meant to fly, God would have given us wings! The automobile? Crazy! It's too noisy and it breaks down too much. Get a horse, you lunatic!

When Jeff Bezos wanted to start an online bookstore in the early 1990s, he had trouble finding anyone who would fund it. Amazon.com worked out very well for him. Or consider the story of Sara Blakely, who cut off the bottom of her pantyhose to create a new product. She then wrote a patent for her footless pantyhose and tried to find someone, anyone, who would support her idea. "Crazy!" everyone said. No takers. Then she finally found a partner, and in 2000 started selling what she called Spanx. Blakely is now on the Forbes World's Billionaires list.

Nearly all creative ideas can sound crazy when first presented. Most people don't have creative imaginations, so most people don't get what the creative is saying. And people tend to be fearful of things they don't understand. That further exacerbates the problem. But if you can't bring in a few people who seem crazy compared to the norm, then you probably aren't going to have a creative organization.

Perhaps Bird was the most creative and crazy person I ever employed. With long arms and legs, he was about 6'9" and tipped the scale at around 150 pounds—none of us had ever seen anyone so skinny. His movements were like those of a bird, thus the nickname.

Bird had one speed: fast. He would run to and from work (a few miles away from his home), except during a rainstorm, at which time he drove a Volkswagen Beetle, each side of which was painted a different color. To watch him get out of it was like watching six circus clowns emerge from a tiny car—it seemed impossible that those long limbs could fit inside, much less find a way out.

Bird turned his office into a combination workshop and workspace, consisting basically of tables built around the perimeter of the walls, with a twenty-square-foot space in the middle where he stood. (The tables were all positioned so he could work at them while standing.)

Bird spoke with a thick Slavic accent and was almost impossible to understand, which meant he couldn't explain his ideas to anyone. But he could prototype. Many of his contraptions were incomprehensible, even with the prototype. But every few months he came up with gold. We were building toys at the time, and he was able to invent functions for our electronic pets that were truly remarkable. For example, he was able to figure out a way to make our cats purr with just thirty cents' worth of parts. Crazy genius!

Like Steve Jobs, Bird found Axlon rather than vice versa. He'd heard that I was the one that would understand his ideas, and so he camped out at my toy company with a box of his stuff until he got an interview with me. (He refused to meet with anyone else.) He stayed until he went back to Croatia.

Steve Jobs himself had crazy ideas. Consider the iPod. At the time of its conception, Apple was having some serious issues with its computers. Plenty of work could have been devoted to improving its operating system. Yet instead, Steve plowed his energy and resources into developing a music player rather than a computer product, something no other computer company had done, or was even thinking about doing. Imagine Dell going into the music business! I know that many people at Apple thought Steve was crazy as a loon when they heard his plans. It worked out. Big time.

Crazy! ideas

"It is quite impossible that the noble organs of human speech could be replaced by ignoble, senseless metal."

> —Jean Bouillaud, member of the French Academy of Sciences, at a demonstration of the phonograph, 1878

"Heavier-than-air flying machines are impossible."

> —Lord Kelvin, president of the British Royal Society, 1895

"The horse is here to stay, but the automobile is only a novelty—a fad."

> —President of the Michigan Savings Bank, advising Henry Ford's lawyer not to invest in the Ford Motor Company, 1903

"I think there is a market for about five computers."

>   —Thomas J. Watson, chairman of the Board of IBM,
>   1943

"Video won't be able to hold onto any market it captures after the first six months. People will soon get tired of staring at a plywood box every night."

>   —Darryl Zanuck, head of 20th Century Fox Studios,
>   1946

"The world potential market for copying machines is 5,000 at most."

>   —IBM, to the eventual founders of Xerox, explaining
>   why the photocopier market was not large enough to
>   justify production, 1959

"There is no reason for any individual to have a computer in their home."

>   —Ken Olsen, president of Digital Equipment
>   Corporation at the Convention of the World Future
>   Society, 1977

I N T R O D U C T I O N
MAKE YOUR WORKPLACE AN ADVERTISEMENT
FOR YOUR COMPANY ADOPT FLEXIBLE PONGS
ADVERTISE CREATIVELY HIRE FOR PASSION
AND INTENSITY IGNORE CREDENTIALS LOOK
FOR HOBBIES USE EMPLOYEES AS RESOURCES
AVOID THE CLONES HIRE THE OBNOXIOUS HIRE
THE CRAZY **FIND THE BULLIED** LOOK FOR THE
LURKERS ASK ABOUT BOOKS SAIL A BOAT HIRE
UNDER YOUR NOSE COMB THROUGH TWEETS
VISIT CREATIVE COMMUNITIES BEWARE OF
POSEURS ASK ODD QUESTIONS CONDUCT DEEP
INTERVIEWS CELEBRATE INSTITUTE A DEGREE OF
ANARCHY PROMOTE PRANKSTERISM SKUNK IT
UP FOSTER FAIRNESS ISOLATE CHAMPION THE
BAD IDEAS CELEBRATE FAILURE REQUIRE RISK
REWARD TURKEYS MENTOR TREAT EMPLOYEES
AS ADULTS CREATE A CREATIVE CHAIN CREATE
A CREATIVE SPACE DESIGNATE A DEMO DAY
ENCOURAGE ADHD PRELOAD LEARN TO
TALK CREATIVE THINK TOYS NEUTRALIZE THE
NAYSAYERS WRITE DOWN OBJECTIONS TAKE
CREATIVES TO CREATIVE PLACES MAKE SOMETHING
FOR THE RICH CHANGE EVERY DAY, EVERY
HOUR THROW THE DICE DUCK PROCESSES
TAKE A RANDOM WALK THROUGH WIKIPEDIA
DON'T COUNT ON ACCOUNTING INVENT
HAPHAZARD HOLIDAYS MIX IT UP GO TO SLEEP
C O N C L U S I O N

11

Many creatives believe in themselves and their own creativity. They were often those kids who knew they were smarter than everyone else in the class—and still believe it. They're often right. That's why they can be so obnoxious (see pong 9).

Many other creatives, however, were the ones who were pushed around and mocked for being different, for having odd ideas, or for dressing strangely. The other kids made fun of them all the time. The teachers tried to knock some sense into them. Their parents despaired of their ever being "normal."

Some of these kids fought back, but many didn't. Nothing makes people conform quicker than the fear of getting hurt, bullied, or mocked. Pain is a great motivator.

As surely as other kids, teachers, and parents can knock the creativity out of children, companies can knock the creativity out of their employees, ruining their self-confidence along the way. That's particularly true if the person's identity is constructed around creativity. It's almost impossible to maintain your sense of self-worth if you propose interesting idea after interesting idea and your company refuses to adopt any—or even, perhaps, entertain any. Worse, the company may mock them.

This response is a form of bullying as bad as the schoolyard variety. How frustrating and unhappy it makes a creative—all those great ideas she thought she would bring to the company have amounted to a heap of nothing, and now she sits around in her office, feeling terrible about her inability to perform.

A great number of companies brag about all the creative people they have on staff. But this is not because they actually experiment with creative ideas. It's because they know it sounds good to *say* they have a creative company, whether or not they let their creatives do anything. Meanwhile, their poor, underutilized creatives are slowly trained into believing that creativity just gets them into trouble. And so, at their next job interview, they downplay their creativity. "I don't want to go through that again," they think. "I'll play it safe this time."

These creatives need to find a job where they can be, well, creative—who they truly are. At some point you will be sitting across from one such person at a job interview. Draw her out. Make her feel at ease. Maybe she wasn't able to accomplish anything at her last job, but get her talking about her creative triumphs before that time. Maybe she won a poetry contest at school, or first prize at a science fair, or was the lead in a local play. She's learned over the years to hide this part of her, which is actually her most valuable and interesting characteristic.

Some of my best employees have come from companies where their talents were totally wasted. I remember one particularly toxic company that put together a little show of their employees' creative ideas. They were never going to put these ideas on the market, but they wanted to show them off to shine a spotlight on their originality. The employees who really excelled at this event were the ones who never got their ideas across at any other time. This demo turned into something of a job fair for these people—all of them were picked off by other employers who saw their full potential.

Warning to companies that refuse to foster their creatives: Don't put on a show to highlight these employees for your competitors.

INTRODUCTION MAKE YOUR WORKPLACE AN ADVERTISEMENT FOR YOUR COMPANY ADOPT FLEXIBLE PONGS ADVERTISE CREATIVELY HIRE FOR PASSION AND INTENSITY IGNORE CREDENTIALS LOOK FOR HOBBIES USE EMPLOYEES AS RESOURCES AVOID THE CLONES HIRE THE OBNOXIOUS HIRE THE CRAZY FIND THE BULLIED **LOOK FOR THE LURKERS** ASK ABOUT BOOKS SAIL A BOAT HIRE UNDER YOUR NOSE COMB THROUGH TWEETS VISIT CREATIVE COMMUNITIES BEWARE OF POSEURS ASK ODD QUESTIONS CONDUCT DEEP INTERVIEWS CELEBRATE INSTITUTE A DEGREE OF ANARCHY PROMOTE PRANKSTERISM SKUNK IT UP FOSTER FAIRNESS ISOLATE CHAMPION THE BAD IDEAS CELEBRATE FAILURE REQUIRE RISK REWARD TURKEYS MENTOR TREAT EMPLOYEES AS ADULTS CREATE A CREATIVE CHAIN CREATE A CREATIVE SPACE DESIGNATE A DEMO DAY ENCOURAGE ADHD PRELOAD LEARN TO TALK CREATIVE THINK TOYS NEUTRALIZE THE NAYSAYERS WRITE DOWN OBJECTIONS TAKE CREATIVESTOCREATIVEPLACESMAKESOMETHING FOR THE RICH CHANGE EVERY DAY, EVERY HOUR THROW THE DICE DUCK PROCESSES TAKE A RANDOM WALK THROUGH WIKIPEDIA DON'T COUNT ON ACCOUNTING INVENT HAPHAZARD HOLIDAYS MIX IT UP GO TO SLEEP CONCLUSION

12

The other day I gave a speech on my new passion, education. Afterward, a handful of people started lurking around the podium, waiting to talk to me, eyes bright with passion but perhaps a little shy.

I hired two of them.

The willingness to get up after a speech, approach the speaker, and tell him how much you enjoyed his ideas speaks volumes. I have a friend in New York media who has hired all of his assistants from the pool of people who've come up after a speech to ask questions.

In fact, many people I know make it a regular practice to meet these lurkers and talk with them. Every company, of whatever size, must put at least some representatives out on the road to talk up the brand and collect lurkers. However, those reps must be compelling. One of Steve Jobs' best traits was that he was an absolutely mesmerizing speaker—people swooned when they heard him. The first time I saw him on stage at a developers' conference, which was later rebroadcast, he was wearing KEEN footwear. KEEN was sold out of that style for months afterward.

The reason lurkers appear is because the speaker, like Steve, has called them up there by virtue of his charisma. Basically, no matter what the topic, every speech from your company's designated speaker is all about selling faith in the brand. (If the company's CEO isn't a good public speaker, then you need to

49

select its public face from lower in the ranks.) If the message is on target and the evangelism is sound, acolytes will appear.

Some of my best hires were lurkers. I picked up my head of franchising for Chuck E. Cheese's at a speech I gave to the National Restaurant Association when a lurker told me that he loved what we were doing and that he was an expert in franchising. He was correct—he did a great job for us. My vice president of sales at Atari, Gene Lipkin, came up to me after a speech, talked to me for a few minutes, and then asked if there was a spot for him. Bingo! A position was filled.

INTRODUCTION MAKE YOUR WORKPLACE AN ADVERTISEMENT FOR YOUR COMPANY ADOPT FLEXIBLE PONGS ADVERTISE CREATIVELY HIRE FOR PASSION AND INTENSITY IGNORE CREDENTIALS LOOK FOR HOBBIES USE EMPLOYEES AS RESOURCES AVOID THE CLONES HIRE THE OBNOXIOUS HIRE THE CRAZY FIND THE BULLIED LOOK FOR THE LURKERS **ASK ABOUT BOOKS** SAIL A BOAT HIRE UNDER YOUR NOSE COMB THROUGH TWEETS VISIT CREATIVE COMMUNITIES BEWARE OF POSEURS ASK ODD QUESTIONS CONDUCT DEEP INTERVIEWS CELEBRATE INSTITUTE A DEGREE OF ANARCHY PROMOTE PRANKSTERISM SKUNK IT UP FOSTER FAIRNESS ISOLATE CHAMPION THE BAD IDEAS CELEBRATE FAILURE REQUIRE RISK REWARD TURKEYS MENTOR TREAT EMPLOYEES AS ADULTS CREATE A CREATIVE CHAIN CREATE A CREATIVE SPACE DESIGNATE A DEMO DAY ENCOURAGE ADHD PRELOAD LEARN TO TALK CREATIVE THINK TOYS NEUTRALIZE THE NAYSAYERS WRITE DOWN OBJECTIONS TAKE CREATIVES TO CREATIVE PLACES MAKE SOMETHING FOR THE RICH CHANGE EVERY DAY, EVERY HOUR THROW THE DICE DUCK PROCESSES TAKE A RANDOM WALK THROUGH WIKIPEDIA DON'T COUNT ON ACCOUNTING INVENT HAPHAZARD HOLIDAYS MIX IT UP GO TO SLEEP CONCLUSION

13

One of the best ways to find creative people is to ask a simple question: "What books do you like?"

I've never met a creative person in my life that didn't respond with enthusiasm to a question about reading habits. For years I've used this question to weed out prospective applicants—those people who come into my office, sit down, and talk grandly about this or that idea, but then look as empty as a blank computer screen when I ask them to list their favorite books.

Each type of employee has different reading interests. I've found that engineers, for example, tend to read science fiction, which is my own favorite genre. Science fiction novels are the training wheels for creative thought: so many ideas from science fiction have become the norm in reality, and many more will become so. Will we all someday employ personal robots? Will there be colonies in space? Will we wear eye implants? Will nanotech medicine repair our bodies? The answer to all of these questions is yes, and for those who read science fiction, these and other predictions are already part of their belief system.

Actually, *which* books people read is not as important as the simple fact that they read at all. (I've known many talented engineers who hated science fiction but loved, say, books on bird watching.) A blatant but often accurate generalization: People who are curious and passionate read. People who are apathetic and indifferent don't.

I remember one particular woman who, during an interview,

told me that she had read every book I had read. So I started mentioning books I hadn't read, and she'd read those too. I didn't know how someone in her late twenties found the time to read so much, but I was so impressed that I hired her right there and assigned her to international marketing, which was having problems. A job with a lot of moving parts benefits from a brain that has a lot of moving parts. It wouldn't be possible to have read that many books without such a brain.

Tip for interviewers: Be ready to ask potential employees for a list of their ten favorite books.

Tip for job seekers: Be ready to volunteer the titles of your ten favorite books. It's very embarrassing when someone says she absolutely loves reading, and then, when asked for some titles, can't name a single one.

Here is my own favorite-book list. It changes from month to month. Actually, from day to day. These just happen to be the ten I might think of if I were asked the question at an interview this minute. Ask me tomorrow for another list.

Hyperion by Dan Simmons

The New World of Mr. Tompkins by George Gamow

Snow Crash by Neal Stephenson

Neuromancer by William Gibson

The Pillars of the Earth by Ken Follett

The Lord of the Rings by J.R.R. Tolkien

Sherlock Holmes (any of them) by Sir Arthur Conan Doyle

The Stranger by Albert Camus

The Essential Kierkegaard by Søren Kierkegaard

The Republic by Plato

INTRODUCTION
MAKE YOUR WORKPLACE AN ADVERTISEMENT
FOR YOUR COMPANY ADOPT FLEXIBLE PONGS
ADVERTISE CREATIVELY HIRE FOR PASSION
AND INTENSITY IGNORE CREDENTIALS LOOK
FOR HOBBIES USE EMPLOYEES AS RESOURCES
AVOID THE CLONES HIRE THE OBNOXIOUS HIRE
THE CRAZY FIND THE BULLIED LOOK FOR THE
LURKERS ASK ABOUT BOOKS **SAIL A BOAT** HIRE
UNDER YOUR NOSE COMB THROUGH TWEETS
VISIT CREATIVE COMMUNITIES BEWARE OF
POSEURS ASK ODD QUESTIONS CONDUCT DEEP
INTERVIEWS CELEBRATE INSTITUTE A DEGREE OF
ANARCHY PROMOTE PRANKSTERISM SKUNK IT
UP FOSTER FAIRNESS ISOLATE CHAMPION THE
BAD IDEAS CELEBRATE FAILURE REQUIRE RISK
REWARD TURKEYS MENTOR TREAT EMPLOYEES
AS ADULTS CREATE A CREATIVE CHAIN CREATE
A CREATIVE SPACE DESIGNATE A DEMO DAY
ENCOURAGE ADHD PRELOAD LEARN TO
TALK CREATIVE THINK TOYS NEUTRALIZE THE
NAYSAYERS WRITE DOWN OBJECTIONS TAKE
CREATIVESTOCREATIVEPLACESMAKESOMETHING
FOR THE RICH CHANGE EVERY DAY, EVERY
HOUR THROW THE DICE DUCK PROCESSES
TAKE A RANDOM WALK THROUGH WIKIPEDIA
DON'T COUNT ON ACCOUNTING INVENT
HAPHAZARD HOLIDAYS MIX IT UP GO TO SLEEP
CONCLUSION

14

Back in the 1970s, I owned a forty-one-foot sailboat. Whenever I became frustrated and had some down time, I sailed. This was before cell phones. Once you were out on a sailboat, you found true isolation, which is very valuable (see pong 26).

But I quickly discovered another of the boat's uses—it was a great way to measure a potential job candidate's character.

On a sailboat, everyone has distinct jobs. One person steers, another keeps watch, another tends the sails, and so on. Observing people as they carried out these tasks always gave me insight into how they reacted in a foreign environment and how well they took instruction.

Occasionally things happen that can be a little scary. Some people become frozen when scared. And if everyone in a scary situation on a sailboat is frightened, they could literally die. I once had a prospective employee on the boat who, when given an easy-to-follow but important order, simply stood still. I did not hire this person, because like it or not, everyone on a boat has joined a team project. You can't sit back and expect other people to save your ass. Even if you're a novice, you have to try, even if you get it wrong. This person was clearly not going to be a good member of our creative team.

If, like most people, you don't sail, consider any number of other hobbies or pastimes you might want to share with a potential employee. A friend of mine who loves to bowl asks people to go with him, whether or not they've bowled before. He's not looking to see how well they play; he's looking to see how they handle a potentially disorienting situation: with grace, humor, and amiability—or with frustration, sulkiness, and poor sportsmanship. The good news here is that life-or-death scenarios seldom arise in a bowling alley.

INTRODUCTION
MAKE YOUR WORKPLACE AN ADVERTISEMENT
FOR YOUR COMPANY ADOPT FLEXIBLE PONGS
ADVERTISE CREATIVELY HIRE FOR PASSION
AND INTENSITY IGNORE CREDENTIALS LOOK
FOR HOBBIES USE EMPLOYEES AS RESOURCES
AVOID THE CLONES HIRE THE OBNOXIOUS HIRE
THE CRAZY FIND THE BULLIED LOOK FOR THE
LURKERS ASK ABOUT BOOKS SAIL A BOAT **HIRE
UNDER YOUR NOSE** COMB THROUGH TWEETS
VISIT CREATIVE COMMUNITIES BEWARE OF
POSEURS ASK ODD QUESTIONS CONDUCT DEEP
INTERVIEWS CELEBRATE INSTITUTE A DEGREE OF
ANARCHY PROMOTE PRANKSTERISM SKUNK IT
UP FOSTER FAIRNESS ISOLATE CHAMPION THE
BAD IDEAS CELEBRATE FAILURE REQUIRE RISK
REWARD TURKEYS MENTOR TREAT EMPLOYEES
AS ADULTS CREATE A CREATIVE CHAIN CREATE
A CREATIVE SPACE DESIGNATE A DEMO DAY
ENCOURAGE ADHD PRELOAD LEARN TO
TALK CREATIVE THINK TOYS NEUTRALIZE THE
NAYSAYERS WRITE DOWN OBJECTIONS TAKE
CREATIVESTOCREATIVEPLACESMAKESOMETHING
FOR THE RICH CHANGE EVERY DAY, EVERY
HOUR THROW THE DICE DUCK PROCESSES
TAKE A RANDOM WALK THROUGH WIKIPEDIA
DON'T COUNT ON ACCOUNTING INVENT
HAPHAZARD HOLIDAYS MIX IT UP GO TO SLEEP
CONCLUSION

15

Watching people doing their jobs outside of your workplace is one of the best ways to find creatives to hire. When I say this, people often laugh. "I just can't walk into another company and sit down and watch," they insist.

Yes, you can. You're just not thinking creatively about where these people may be found. Creative people aren't necessarily working in creative jobs. The problem with our workforce (and hiring practices) is that creatives often can't find jobs—or at least, they can't find jobs in the field in which they most want to work. Being passionate and interesting, in itself, doesn't pay the rent, so passionate, interesting people often work at dull jobs because no one else wants to hire them.

I've often hired people who caught my attention by being creative at their jobs. One of the best hires I ever made was a waitress at a California Pizza Kitchen restaurant. She was funny, she turned all of my feeble attempts at humor into real comedy, and she made everyone around her feel terrific. In awe, my whole family watched this woman as if she had a 10,000-watt spotlight trained on her. I hired her right then and there to develop some innovative marketing programs. She turned out to be spectacular, pouring the same positive energy that made her an amazing waitress into her new job with me.

Another time, I was shopping for camping equipment at a North Face store in Palo Alto, California. The young man who helped me was so knowledgeable about gear, and so passionate about camping itself, that talking to him was a joy. It's rare to meet a salesperson who is simultaneously technically proficient, charming, and entertaining. I knew immediately that I wanted him working for Chuck E. Cheese's. We placed him in customer service, as his talent for that was obvious, and he rose to the top of the department in just a year.

Too often people see only what they expect to see. If you expect to see only a waitress, that's all you'll see. If you look at everyone as a possible addition to your staff, then suddenly the world of possibilities has exploded. Take off your blinders. Creative people are all around you. Don't stop looking just because you're off work or taking care of some errands. Some of the most creative people you'll find are hiding in plain sight.

Attention job seekers: No matter what type of job you are currently holding, as long as one other person is watching you, you are on stage. You never know when someone will come along who may offer you your next job.

Actually, you may not even need to leave the office to find creatives hiding in ordinary jobs. Just because they've gotten in the door at your company doesn't mean they are well placed—often, they're totally miscast. One of the best ways to find them is to practice Management by Walking Around. This means that when you have a problem, you get up from behind your desk and go talk to the receptionist, talk to the woman in accounting, talk to the guy in sales.

Why? For one thing, you're including people who are normally ignored in the larger picture, and that in itself is good. But often, you'll get a new perspective on the problem from someone who knows your business well. Diverse inputs are as necessary for creative growth as water is for life.

Expectations drive actions. If you have an organization where you don't expect anyone to be creative, they won't be. If you create one where creativity is a given, they will rise to that expectation.

Hiring on the sidelines

For me, one of the pleasures of life has always been attending my children's athletic events. I'm proud of my kids, whether they win or lose. But I've also noticed that a lot of very smart people are doing the same thing I'm doing. And they're equally bored. Yes, there's little worse than having your kid decide he or she wants to be on a swim team, because swim meets are interminable and massively dull. There you are, sitting in the bleachers, while a bunch of kids, none of whom you can tell from the other at that distance, are chugging along in a swimming pool as fast as they can.

To alleviate that boredom, you end up spending the whole time talking with the other parents. Typically, I'll talk technology, and in some cases, offer people jobs on the spot.

For instance, at one meet back in the 1970s, I started talking to the guy sitting next to me, a man named Bob Brown. I asked him what he did, and he replied that he designed custom chips. One topic led to another, and soon we were discussing the gaming business. This was at a time when a lot of people were anti-war, and we agreed that designing chips for games was more fun than designing them for military applications. Before the meet was over, I'd hired Bob, an excellent engineer who could design just about anything.

Never stop thinking of places to find and hire good people.

INTRODUCTION
MAKE YOUR WORKPLACE AN ADVERTISEMENT
FOR YOUR COMPANY ADOPT FLEXIBLE PONGS
ADVERTISE CREATIVELY HIRE FOR PASSION
AND INTENSITY IGNORE CREDENTIALS LOOK
FOR HOBBIES USE EMPLOYEES AS RESOURCES
AVOID THE CLONES HIRE THE OBNOXIOUS HIRE
THE CRAZY FIND THE BULLIED LOOK FOR THE
LURKERS ASK ABOUT BOOKS SAIL A BOAT HIRE
UNDER YOUR NOSE **COMB THROUGH TWEETS**
VISIT CREATIVE COMMUNITIES BEWARE OF
POSEURS ASK ODD QUESTIONS CONDUCT DEEP
INTERVIEWS CELEBRATE INSTITUTE A DEGREE OF
ANARCHY PROMOTE PRANKSTERISM SKUNK IT
UP FOSTER FAIRNESS ISOLATE CHAMPION THE
BAD IDEAS CELEBRATE FAILURE REQUIRE RISK
REWARD TURKEYS MENTOR TREAT EMPLOYEES
AS ADULTS CREATE A CREATIVE CHAIN CREATE
A CREATIVE SPACE DESIGNATE A DEMO DAY
ENCOURAGE ADHD PRELOAD LEARN TO
TALK CREATIVE THINK TOYS NEUTRALIZE THE
NAYSAYERS WRITE DOWN OBJECTIONS TAKE
CREATIVESTOCREATIVEPLACESMAKESOMETHING
FOR THE RICH CHANGE EVERY DAY, EVERY
HOUR THROW THE DICE DUCK PROCESSES
TAKE A RANDOM WALK THROUGH WIKIPEDIA
DON'T COUNT ON ACCOUNTING INVENT
HAPHAZARD HOLIDAYS MIX IT UP GO TO SLEEP
CONCLUSION

16

The Internet has made it much easier to find, and learn about, potential job applicants. But I still don't hear about HR departments using the Internet for anything other than to google applicants' names in hopes of finding embarrassing YouTube videos of them throwing up or Facebook photos of them passed out.

There are better ways to find creatives. For example, one of the best is to randomly read Twitter feeds.

When Twitter first appeared, it seemed as though it might amount to nothing more than a chance for people to announce they'd just brushed their teeth or eaten a nice meal. What it's turned into, however, is a kind of hyper index.

Think of Twitter as an infinite number of headlines. If a particular subject area meshes with your company's mission, Twitter provides a non-curated platform you can use to find people who are posting creative and smart tweets about your topic of interest.

A lot of these people are creatives yearning to be free, and they are using Twitter as their outlet, their medium of expression. They may be stuck in a bad job, or unemployed, but they're not watching television or eating junk food all day. Their creativity is overflowing onto the web.

Let's say I am looking for a public-relations person who can deal with technical introductions. I would search Twitter for some technical introductions, see who tweeted them, click on their profiles and, by looking at the rest of their tweets, determine their intelligence and their possible fit within my company.

I randomly search Twitter every week. Because I'm starting a new educational venture, I check to see who might be saying something original and bright on the subject. If I find someone, I follow him, he follows me, and soon we may have a dialogue going. I expect to be hiring a great many people in the next few years. Some of them will come off of Twitter feeds.

Mind you, like all pongs, this one is not foolproof. I once found a prolific and elegant tweeter. We connected, and soon I was receiving an email from him every day, full of imaginative new ideas. I thought he was the smartest guy I'd (almost) ever met and so, sight unseen, I offered him a job and flew him to California to work on software. It turns out that yes, he was full of ideas. But he could not execute any of them. He was a great big tweet with nothing behind it. He lasted six months.

INTRODUCTION
MAKE YOUR WORKPLACE AN ADVERTISEMENT
FOR YOUR COMPANY ADOPT FLEXIBLE PONGS
ADVERTISE CREATIVELY HIRE FOR PASSION
AND INTENSITY IGNORE CREDENTIALS LOOK
FOR HOBBIES USE EMPLOYEES AS RESOURCES
AVOID THE CLONES HIRE THE OBNOXIOUS HIRE
THE CRAZY FIND THE BULLIED LOOK FOR THE
LURKERS ASK ABOUT BOOKS SAIL A BOAT HIRE
UNDER YOUR NOSE COMB THROUGH TWEETS

VISIT CREATIVE COMMUNITIES BEWARE OF
POSEURS ASK ODD QUESTIONS CONDUCT DEEP
INTERVIEWS CELEBRATE INSTITUTE A DEGREE OF
ANARCHY PROMOTE PRANKSTERISM SKUNK IT
UP FOSTER FAIRNESS ISOLATE CHAMPION THE
BAD IDEAS CELEBRATE FAILURE REQUIRE RISK
REWARD TURKEYS MENTOR TREAT EMPLOYEES
AS ADULTS CREATE A CREATIVE CHAIN CREATE
A CREATIVE SPACE DESIGNATE A DEMO DAY
ENCOURAGE ADHD PRELOAD LEARN TO
TALK CREATIVE THINK TOYS NEUTRALIZE THE
NAYSAYERS WRITE DOWN OBJECTIONS TAKE
CREATIVES TO CREATIVE PLACES MAKE SOMETHING
FOR THE RICH CHANGE EVERY DAY, EVERY
HOUR THROW THE DICE DUCK PROCESSES
TAKE A RANDOM WALK THROUGH WIKIPEDIA
DON'T COUNT ON ACCOUNTING INVENT
HAPHAZARD HOLIDAYS MIX IT UP GO TO SLEEP
CONCLUSION

17

Creative communities have existed wherever there has been imagination. Creatives, like misery, love company. In ancient Greece the great thinker Pythagoras established a community at Croton, a Greek colony in southern Italy, where followers performed religious rites and discussed philosophy. Many centuries later during the Renaissance, Florence was a creative center for writers, artists, and musicians, giving the world some of its most enduring works. The coffeehouses of Vienna in the decades leading up to World War I were filled with brilliant people often inspired by mutual interactions. There, composer Gustav Mahler was psychoanalyzed by Sigmund Freud and Gustav Klimt painted a portrait of Ludwig Wittgenstein's sister for her wedding. Similarly, following the war, artists from all over the world—including Samuel Beckett, Ernest Hemingway, James Joyce, Henry Miller, Ezra Pound, and Gertrude Stein—gathered in Paris, where informal networks of artists, publishers, and bookstore owners depended upon one another for their livelihoods as well as for inspiration.

You don't have to go back in time to find creative communities. They're always around, whether formal, planned gatherings or off-the-cuff get-togethers. I've seen groups that range from a few people meeting to talk about science fiction to large numbers of people convening to build fantastical projects. And whenever or wherever you find these communities, you'll find potential employees.

Being an engineering type, the first such groups I joined were of like-minded engineers. The Hackers Conference, a gathering of some of the brightest minds in technology, is the most memorable. I saw things there I couldn't otherwise have imagined, such as the first hacked cell phone. Another time a young man charged up a great big capacitor, and then discharged it through a pickle. The liquid in the pickle atomized, and suddenly a thin layer of pickle surrounded us in a twenty-foot circle. The Hackers Conference was also the place where I first saw the effects of a microwave oven on a compact disc.

At Atari, we would send employees out to any number of these conferences and/or communities to make sure that people were familiar with our brand and our ongoing projects. While there, our employees often picked up interesting ideas and made connections with potential influencers who were impressed that our company was aware of their grassroots efforts.

Some other creative communities to visit:

Burning Man, out in the Nevada desert. I often attend this weeklong event, where people come to do whatever they can think of doing. I've seen and heard everything from poetry in a pup tent to space-age synthesizer music in the air. At almost every camp there's a bar; to give you a taste of the environment, a sign in one of them read: "No discussion of quantum mechanics without a PhD or an understanding of the mathematics." Really creative people come here. It's an employment center disguised as a festival.

Mindshare is one of my favorites: It's a monthly salon and networking event that convenes people from different backgrounds, including artists, scientists and technology experts. Mindshare, whose tagline is "enlightened debauchery," features short-form presentations and a well-stocked bar. The events now take place all over the country and generally feature four speakers talking about anything and everything, including belly dancing, tai chi, electrical implants, the environment, future trends, and new inventions.

METal is a Los Angeles group with a great collection of talent that meets Saturday mornings for breakfast and a talk. Attendees are passionate enough about life to get out of bed on a Saturday morning, drive many miles, and share ideas.

The Prairie Festival takes place in the middle of Kansas but attracts more than a thousand people willing to spend a weekend outdoors learning about agriculture, sustainability, and the environment. If I were hiring in this field, I'd head out to Salina, Kansas, in October with a hundred business cards.

The Maker Movement's Maker Faire started with an O'Reilly Media publication, *Make* magazine, that featured articles on topics such as building a guitar out of a cigar box and creating your own pulse-jet engine. O'Reilly found out that readers were building many of these projects and wanted to show them to someone else, so they established Maker Faire at the San Mateo County fairgrounds. People came from all over the country to show their hobbies—the place was packed with innovators! What a great place to recruit employees. These people had discovered their passion, gotten off their butt, created a project, taken it across town or cross country, and proudly showed it off. They are the types who, instead of watching television twelve hours a day, might be able to make you a new television that does things you couldn't possibly imagine. The Maker Faire is now held many times throughout the year in locations worldwide.

BIL is an "unconference" held over three days in Long Beach, California. Anyone can attend for a donation of any amount. Attendees, called "Bilders," gather informally to hear talks such as "How to be a Successful Heretic." BIL began in 2008, and its tagline is "Minds Set Free." Topics range from robotics to DIY biology.

The PICNIC Festival is a two-day European event that explores the intersection of creativity and innovation. In 2012, 3,000 creatives from multiple fields—business, government, education and others—attended. The theme of the 2012 event, held in Amsterdam, was "New Ownership: The Shift from Top-Down to Bottom-Up." Events included lectures, interactive debates and discussions, start-up competitions, and even matchmaking activities.

INTRODUCTION MAKE YOUR WORKPLACE AN ADVERTISEMENT FOR YOUR COMPANY ADOPT FLEXIBLE PONGS ADVERTISE CREATIVELY HIRE FOR PASSION AND INTENSITY IGNORE CREDENTIALS LOOK FOR HOBBIES USE EMPLOYEES AS RESOURCES AVOID THE CLONES HIRE THE OBNOXIOUS HIRE THE CRAZY FIND THE BULLIED LOOK FOR THE LURKERS ASK ABOUT BOOKS SAIL A BOAT HIRE UNDER YOUR NOSE COMB THROUGH TWEETS VISIT CREATIVE COMMUNITIES **BEWARE OF POSEURS** ASK ODD QUESTIONS CONDUCT DEEP INTERVIEWS CELEBRATE INSTITUTE A DEGREE OF ANARCHY PROMOTE PRANKSTERISM SKUNK IT UP FOSTER FAIRNESS ISOLATE CHAMPION THE BAD IDEAS CELEBRATE FAILURE REQUIRE RISK REWARD TURKEYS MENTOR TREAT EMPLOYEES AS ADULTS CREATE A CREATIVE CHAIN CREATE A CREATIVE SPACE DESIGNATE A DEMO DAY ENCOURAGE ADHD PRELOAD LEARN TO TALK CREATIVE THINK TOYS NEUTRALIZE THE NAYSAYERS WRITE DOWN OBJECTIONS TAKE CREATIVESTOCREATIVEPLACESMAKESOMETHING FOR THE RICH CHANGE EVERY DAY, EVERY HOUR THROW THE DICE DUCK PROCESSES TAKE A RANDOM WALK THROUGH WIKIPEDIA DON'T COUNT ON ACCOUNTING INVENT HAPHAZARD HOLIDAYS MIX IT UP GO TO SLEEP CONCLUSION

18

This book's basic readership is people who want their company to be more creative. My fear is that some readers will use it differently: as a guide to being a phony. After all, I'm giving them a whole bunch of ideas on how to act like a creative.

One of the biggest lessons I've learned over the years is that the business world (and by extension, the world itself) is filled with poseurs. These people are quite clever at figuring out what you want them to say, and then saying it exactly the way you want to hear it.

I first learned about the omnipresence of phonies during the early days of Atari. The custom chip business was very difficult and time consuming. And because it could take at least a year to get a completed custom chip working, a whole cadre of people posing as chip designers would always find ways to leave the company or get fired before the chip ever worked. Steve Jobs once told me that there were many employees at Apple who never got a single chip working. I told him it was the same at Atari. These people were able to go from job to job to job, doing something that seemed creative but yielding zero output. I remember one guy whose nickname became "I Almost Have It." Every time we'd ask if his chip was ready, that's what he'd say.

You have to be very wary of poseurs. So how do you recognize them?

For one thing, don't rely solely on credentials in hiring (see pong 5). In the chip world, for example, someone can have terrific credentials in chip design without any ability to get a chip engineered. Such poseurs know how to build up a terrific-looking résumé. You'll soon find out it's their major talent.

Second, when you're interviewing prospective employees, try this trick: Ask second and third questions about a topic after they've responded so fluently to your opening question. Poseurs are generally fluent in surface jargon. Get them to go into greater depth about a subject and you may well find them starting to lose that verbal acuity.

For example, let's say you're looking for a marketing expert. These days, marketers are all about analytics. Any poseur for a marketing job can come in and start spouting about the importance of analytics. Stop him right there and ask, "Which ones are the most important?" Then say, "What do you think is a cost per lead from Google? When you are putting together a marketing program, what do you consider a good outcome?"

In other words, ask judgment questions. Ask a lot of them. If you're not an expert in the field yourself, get someone to prepare a dozen questions for you.

Also, a lot of people know the *how* of a job but they don't necessarily understand the *why*. "So you collected all analytics," you ask. "Why did you do it? Why are they important? Why did you use these analytics to increase the outcome?"

I've found that having played poker helps me when I ask tough questions like these. I was a good player, relying on the "tells," or facial expressions and body language that often give away a person's hand, which are very subtle. For example, according to recent research from Northeastern University, Massachusetts Institute of Technology, and Cornell University, one specific cluster of non-verbal cues is especially associated with lying: hand touching, face touching, crossing arms, and leaning away. The studies found that none of these cues alone predicted a lie, but when taken together they became an accurate signifier of deception.

The poseur's fundamental skill is the bluff. For some reason they don't feel a need to go past that, which is why they are easily unmasked. At Atari, I once hired two people who came from Hewlett-Packard. At the time, HP was considered the best company in the field. If you'd landed one of its executives, you felt pretty lucky. And these guys were like butter: so smooth, so polished, so frictionless. It turned out that they didn't know how to do anything *except* shine at an interview, and, once on the job, take credit for what their underlings did.

All of us have been taken in by poseurs at one point or another. The trick is to learn from the experience rather than endlessly repeat it.

I N T R O D U C T I O N
MAKE YOUR WORKPLACE AN ADVERTISEMENT
FOR YOUR COMPANY ADOPT FLEXIBLE PONGS
ADVERTISE CREATIVELY HIRE FOR PASSION
AND INTENSITY IGNORE CREDENTIALS LOOK
FOR HOBBIES USE EMPLOYEES AS RESOURCES
AVOID THE CLONES HIRE THE OBNOXIOUS HIRE
THE CRAZY FIND THE BULLIED LOOK FOR THE
LURKERS ASK ABOUT BOOKS SAIL A BOAT HIRE
UNDER YOUR NOSE COMB THROUGH TWEETS
VISIT CREATIVE COMMUNITIES BEWARE OF
POSEURS **ASK ODD QUESTIONS** *CONDUCT DEEP*
INTERVIEWS CELEBRATE INSTITUTE A DEGREE OF
ANARCHY PROMOTE PRANKSTERISM SKUNK IT
UP FOSTER FAIRNESS ISOLATE CHAMPION THE
BAD IDEAS CELEBRATE FAILURE REQUIRE RISK
REWARD TURKEYS MENTOR TREAT EMPLOYEES
AS ADULTS CREATE A CREATIVE CHAIN CREATE
A CREATIVE SPACE DESIGNATE A DEMO DAY
ENCOURAGE ADHD PRELOAD LEARN TO
TALK CREATIVE THINK TOYS NEUTRALIZE THE
NAYSAYERS WRITE DOWN OBJECTIONS TAKE
CREATIVES TO CREATIVE PLACES MAKE SOMETHING
FOR THE RICH CHANGE EVERY DAY, EVERY
HOUR THROW THE DICE DUCK PROCESSES
TAKE A RANDOM WALK THROUGH WIKIPEDIA
DON'T COUNT ON ACCOUNTING INVENT
HAPHAZARD HOLIDAYS MIX IT UP GO TO SLEEP
C O N C L U S I O N

19

Most people conduct interviews by asking the same boring questions over and over. "Where did you go to school?" "What experience do you have in the field?" "Do you have good references?" "Are you looking forward to working for us?" These questions do not help you find creative people. They can barely keep people awake.

If you are looking to hire interesting employees, ask interesting questions. Odd ones, weird ones, random ones, ones that help you see how someone's mind works, not ones that show you how well they can recite their résumé back to you. The questions don't have to be answerable. You're not there to get real answers to real problems. You're there to witness how a prospective employee's mind works.

I often ask interviewees at lunch how many pieces of gum are stuck under the table. Obviously, I don't know the answer. Neither do they. In fact, I don't care what the answer is. What I want to hear is how they handle the question.

For example, if someone says, "How in the world would I know that?" and moves on, she's not going to work for me. But if she says, "I don't know, but I can see that several people have walked into the restaurant chewing gum, and yet no one is chewing gum while eating, so at least a few of them probably stuck their gum somewhere. For some of them, under the table is the best place. I also see that the café isn't very clean, so the wait staff probably never checks. So I bet there might be, say, three?"

It doesn't matter if she's right (because there may be other variables that neither of us knows). What matters is that she's showing you her mind: the way she thinks, calculates, imagines, and guesses. (By the way, these kinds of questions about approximations, and the ability to justify such estimates, are known as Fermi problems, named after Italian-American physicist Enrico Fermi, who was renowned for his ability to make such approximations without a great deal of information available.)

Taking a different tack, one of my favorite questions for engineers is, "Have you ever done any plumbing?" People may look at you a little strangely when you ask that. But the good candidates will say yes, and then talk about it. That's a good sign. No one (except actual plumbers) ever takes a class on plumbing, so it's the intuitive problem solvers who've tackled the job. That's the person I want working for me.

Some other odd questions I have asked:

What is a mole? (It can be a brown spot on the skin, a spy, a burrowing rodent, or a measure of quantity in chemistry—6.022 times 10 to the 23rd power, also known as Avogadro's constant.)

Is an easy game or a hard game more fun? (Oddly, people often can't figure out how to answer this one.)

What is the most annoying thing in your life? (My favorite answer: "This question.")

Why do track events run counter-clockwise? (No one really knows, but there have been a lot of great guesses.)

If a baseball player hits a home run over the fence, but then dies before running the bases, does the home run count? (Yes, if a pinch runner takes his place.)

What's the opposite of a table? (Nothing, as far as I know. Certainly not a chair.)

I also like to ask these riddles:

1. Three women are standing next to each other in bathing suits. Two of them are sad. The other one is happy. The happy one is crying. The sad ones are smiling. Why?

2. What is the order of these numbers: 8, 5, 4, 9, 1, 7, 6, 3, 2?

3. Peter was 15 years old in 1990 and he was 10 years old in 1995—how can that be?

4. At a recent competition, the contestants had to hold something. The winner was quadriplegic. What did he hold?

5. A girl is walking down a road with three friends. One is an animal, one is a vegetable, and one is a mineral. What's the girl's name?

The answers are on page 228, but remember, it's not about the answers. It's about hearing how job applicants arrive at their answers.

INTRODUCTION MAKE YOUR WORKPLACE AN ADVERTISEMENT FOR YOUR COMPANY ADOPT FLEXIBLE PONGS ADVERTISE CREATIVELY HIRE FOR PASSION AND INTENSITY IGNORE CREDENTIALS LOOK FOR HOBBIES USE EMPLOYEES AS RESOURCES AVOID THE CLONES HIRE THE OBNOXIOUS HIRE THE CRAZY FIND THE BULLIED LOOK FOR THE LURKERS ASK ABOUT BOOKS SAIL A BOAT HIRE UNDER YOUR NOSE COMB THROUGH TWEETS VISIT CREATIVE COMMUNITIES BEWARE OF POSEURS ASK ODD QUESTIONS **CONDUCT DEEP INTERVIEWS** CELEBRATE INSTITUTE A DEGREE OF ANARCHY PROMOTE PRANKSTERISM SKUNK IT UP FOSTER FAIRNESS ISOLATE CHAMPION THE BAD IDEAS CELEBRATE FAILURE REQUIRE RISK REWARD TURKEYS MENTOR TREAT EMPLOYEES AS ADULTS CREATE A CREATIVE CHAIN CREATE A CREATIVE SPACE DESIGNATE A DEMO DAY ENCOURAGE ADHD PRELOAD LEARN TO TALK CREATIVE THINK TOYS NEUTRALIZE THE NAYSAYERS WRITE DOWN OBJECTIONS TAKE CREATIVESTOCREATIVEPLACESMAKESOMETHING FOR THE RICH CHANGE EVERY DAY, EVERY HOUR THROW THE DICE DUCK PROCESSES TAKE A RANDOM WALK THROUGH WIKIPEDIA DON'T COUNT ON ACCOUNTING INVENT HAPHAZARD HOLIDAYS MIX IT UP GO TO SLEEP CONCLUSION

20

When you're conducting interviews, don't ask standard questions, but don't ask shallow ones, either. Don't let people off the hook when they fumble or try to move on to another subject. Go deep. Ask a new question based on their previous response for more granularity. If an interviewee is talking about a project she's working on at another company, ask for details about it, making sure that you focus on what she actually did. People often use the royal "we" when talking about their experience, and although the project might have turned out very well, their particular involvement in it may have been minimal or even nonexistent. She may have been working at the company when the Amazing Widget 450 was being built, but she might have been swabbing out the restrooms.

Flesh out her claims by asking detailed questions, e.g., "When you worked on the Widget 450, what were you responsible for exactly?" If she says she was part of the team that created its amazing marketing slogan, dig in as far as you can. What was her specific contribution, her thinking, her alternative ideas? Why did she like the slogan she suggested, what were the slogans others offered, which parts of those slogans did she like and dislike? Do not stop. Just keep digging.

One of three things will happen. If it turns out that she wasn't so involved after all, you'll watch her make stuff up on the fly. If she wasn't that involved and she can't invent on the fly, that's also good to know. Or if she really was very involved, she'll give you real information about the process at a deep level.

The goal is to ignore the résumé and use the interview to ask as many probing questions as possible.

In the process, don't be looking to find a round employee to fit into a round hole. Find a talented person and then create a position that fits her.

What you want is a collection of amazing people. And if you have a collection of amazing people, they will accomplish amazing things.

KEEPING AND NURTURING THE NEXT STEVE JOBS

SECTION TWO

Okay. You've done all your work. You've thought about where to find the creatives, you've interviewed them, and you've managed to lure them into your company.

Now what?

As you'll see, it isn't enough just to hire the next Steve Jobses. There's no point in adding these people to your staff if you're not going to do anything with them. You have to keep them happy, fulfilled, and feeling as though they are truly a valuable part of the team. Too many times employers struggle to find creative people but, once they have them, don't let them flourish. For some, this oversight is simply mismanagement—the company doesn't know how to take advantage of its creative staff. For others, it is a strategy: Keep the best people away from the company's competitors by hiring them, and then file them away where no one can find them. In the long run, however, this strategy is not a sustainable approach. Sooner or later, these poor creatives will escape their prison inside your corridors of cubicles and find places that will nourish them—and profit from their innovations.

As I've mentioned, one of the most creative engineers I ever met was Al Alcorn, who was pivotal in Atari's success. After I sold Atari to Warner in 1976, Al became a Warner employee. While there, he came up with one terrific idea after another, especially in the area of hand-held games that were very cool and could have been enormously profitable.

None of his ideas ever saw the light of day at Warner. No one above him was creative enough to understand Al's potential, meaning no one at the company was able to recognize his creativity and profit from it. Warner was so busy trying to make more money out of Atari 2600 cartridges that they couldn't see that the 2600 was, in fact, losing its edge. They simply weren't open to all the new ideas Al kept presenting them.

Eventually Al became so frustrated that he left to become an Apple fellow. However, during that period, John Scully was running Apple and the company was foundering. So Al took off again for Silicon Gaming, which did understand his potential and did extremely well by him.

The following thirty-one pongs will help you help the creatives in your organization become the most creative employees they can be—for their benefit, and for yours.

INTRODUCTION MAKE YOUR WORKPLACE AN ADVERTISEMENT FOR YOUR COMPANY ADOPT FLEXIBLE PONGS ADVERTISE CREATIVELY HIRE FOR PASSION AND INTENSITY IGNORE CREDENTIALS LOOK FOR HOBBIES USE EMPLOYEES AS RESOURCES AVOID THE CLONES HIRE THE OBNOXIOUS HIRE THE CRAZY FIND THE BULLIED LOOK FOR THE LURKERS ASK ABOUT BOOKS SAIL A BOAT HIRE UNDER YOUR NOSE COMB THROUGH TWEETS VISIT CREATIVE COMMUNITIES BEWARE OF POSEURS ASK ODD QUESTIONS CONDUCT DEEP INTERVIEWS CELEBRATE INSTITUTE A DEGREE OF ANARCHY PROMOTE PRANKSTERISM SKUNK IT UP FOSTER FAIRNESS ISOLATE CHAMPION THE BAD IDEAS **CELEBRATE** FAILURE REQUIRE RISK REWARD TURKEYS MENTOR TREAT EMPLOYEES AS ADULTS CREATE A CREATIVE CHAIN CREATE A CREATIVE SPACE DESIGNATE A DEMO DAY ENCOURAGE ADHD PRELOAD LEARN TO TALK CREATIVE THINK TOYS NEUTRALIZE THE NAYSAYERS WRITE DOWN OBJECTIONS TAKE CREATIVESTOCREATIVEPLACESMAKESOMETHING FOR THE RICH CHANGE EVERY DAY, EVERY HOUR THROW THE DICE DUCK PROCESSES TAKE A RANDOM WALK THROUGH WIKIPEDIA DON'T COUNT ON ACCOUNTING INVENT HAPHAZARD HOLIDAYS MIX IT UP GO TO SLEEP CONCLUSION

21

One of the best ways to keep creatives happy is to make some happiness happen. One of the best—and most cost effective—ways to do that is to throw an inexpensive party. Yes, a party. If your company can institutionalize a regular episode of genuine, collegial fun, you can create an environment where interesting people want to work—and play.

At Atari we always made sure that our employees had an opportunity to let off a little steam. Officially, the idea was that parties were to take place only when we hit our sales quota, but because we always hit quota, every other Friday we held a kegger with pizza on the back loading dock. The price: less than five hundred dollars. The result: a reputation for being a great place to work.

There was another agenda in having these festivities (besides being an advertisement for the company—see pong 1). The celebration was actually about creating informal lines of communication. Having a party lessens any sense that the company takes itself too seriously, but the real deal is that at parties, people talk to each other more freely and more candidly than while lurking in their cubicles—especially if they've had a little bit to drink. Ideas that might never be mentioned in the office because people were self-conscious about offering radical ideas were often brought up at our blasts. After a few beers, inhibitions often vanish.

These events worked so well that we took the idea further and occasionally threw costume parties—not only because they were fun, but because wearing costumes allows you to become who you want to be instead of who you think you should be. Hiding behind spotted animal outfits and super-hero masks makes people less self-conscious and more willing to speak up about problems—and to offer creative solutions. In other words, parties allow people to speak as themselves instead of in their carefully constructed business personas.

We also found that people sometimes came up with wonderful ideas when we asked them to stop thinking so hard and relax. There's science behind this thinking: When you're constantly working on a specific problem, originality often stops flowing. It's now thought that your conscious brain can handle no more than seven or eight things at a time, but in the background, scores of additional thoughts and concepts are floating around your mind. (Bestselling author and neuroscientist David Eagleman calls the background chatter "zombie programs.") When you relax, some of those otherwise not-so-accessible thoughts rush to the surface; therein may lie the solution to the problem you couldn't force your brain to uncover (see pong 36).

Our attitude was that we never knew when creativity was going to strike—and at our parties it did all the time. At one particularly good bash held in our game room, people were playing one of our driving games. Everyone commented on how much more fun it would be if they could play against each other simultaneously, so one of the engineers quickly came up with an impromptu method of lashing eight of the games together. Suddenly the driving game went from a solitary experience to a social one.

It seemed an obvious move, but no one had thought about doing this before. We immediately put the game into production and called it *Indy 8*. *Indy 8* may well have earned more money than any of our other games. In fact, there was one particular *Indy 8* machine at Disney World reputed to earn one million dollars a year, one quarter at a time (or rather, eight quarters at a time).

No one had ever thought of an eight-player game before, and if this particular man hadn't been having a good time at our party, it might never have existed.

Many other companies practice the Celebrate pong successfully, using their events to keep employees happy and increase productivity. For example, TicketKick, a company that helps Californians deal with their traffic citations, has a variety of people-pleasing tricks, such as offering personal growth classes, allowances for office decoration, and group outings when company goals are met. New employees are treated to steakhouse dinners and given tickets to Disneyland. Vans, the successful shoe and apparel manufacturer, has raffled off trips to Hawaii and sent design teams to Palm Springs, California. It also decks out its family picnics with bounce houses and zip lines. The crown jewel of the company's headquarters in Cypress, California, is a skate bowl used for testing products as well as for blowing off steam. Similarly, San Francisco's Benefit Cosmetics offers a wide variety of celebratory events including monthly theme parties, ice-cream socials, and group trips to baseball games.

One other advantage of the celebration: people's tongues loosen. For example, despite Atari's best efforts, we occasionally hired a few toxic managers, and our celebrations were generally the only place where anyone was willing to let us know about them. Several times, this is how I discovered a manager was stealing; none of his reports had the nerve to tell me until they had a beer in hand and several more in their stomach.

The best story to come out of a beer bust was the following: The wife of an employee showed up at a party and told us her husband, who worked in the purchasing department, was robbing us blind. He'd been buying tools through his brother, who was doubling the cost and taking the profit. The woman had decided to rat him out when she came to meet her husband at one of our parties and found him having sex with one of his employees.

INTRODUCTION
MAKE YOUR WORKPLACE AN ADVERTISEMENT
FOR YOUR COMPANY ADOPT FLEXIBLE PONGS
ADVERTISE CREATIVELY HIRE FOR PASSION
AND INTENSITY IGNORE CREDENTIALS LOOK
FOR HOBBIES USE EMPLOYEES AS RESOURCES
AVOID THE CLONES HIRE THE OBNOXIOUS HIRE
THE CRAZY FIND THE BULLIED LOOK FOR THE
LURKERS ASK ABOUT BOOKS SAIL A BOAT HIRE
UNDER YOUR NOSE COMB THROUGH TWEETS
VISIT CREATIVE COMMUNITIES BEWARE OF
POSEURS ASK ODD QUESTIONS CONDUCT DEEP
INTERVIEWS CELEBRATE **INSTITUTE A DEGREE OF
ANARCHY** PROMOTE PRANKSTERISM SKUNK IT
UP FOSTER FAIRNESS ISOLATE CHAMPION THE
BAD IDEAS CELEBRATE FAILURE REQUIRE RISK
REWARD TURKEYS MENTOR TREAT EMPLOYEES
AS ADULTS CREATE A CREATIVE CHAIN CREATE
A CREATIVE SPACE DESIGNATE A DEMO DAY
ENCOURAGE ADHD PRELOAD LEARN TO
TALK CREATIVE THINK TOYS NEUTRALIZE THE
NAYSAYERS WRITE DOWN OBJECTIONS TAKE
CREATIVESTOCREATIVEPLACESMAKESOMETHING
FOR THE RICH CHANGE EVERY DAY, EVERY
HOUR THROW THE DICE DUCK PROCESSES
TAKE A RANDOM WALK THROUGH WIKIPEDIA
DON'T COUNT ON ACCOUNTING INVENT
HAPHAZARD HOLIDAYS MIX IT UP GO TO SLEEP
CONCLUSION

22

Parties (see pong 21) serve still another creative function. There are few obstacles to achieving creativity in a company more intransigent than a strictly vertical organization. The more horizontal the company's chain of command, the fewer steps from creator to CEO, the better off the company is, creatively speaking.

The beauty of parties is that they are instant hierarchy levelers—they provide an atmosphere in which anyone can communicate with anyone. Assistants can talk to executives, junior management can gossip with senior management, secretaries can chat with the chairman of the board.

At every company I founded, I did whatever was necessary to avoid an overly hierarchical organization. Hierarchy means having managers, and sub-managers, and sub-sub-managers. Basically, when you give people the title of manager, you are enabling them to say no. You want as few people saying no in the company as possible (see pongs 40 and 41).

The better model is the horizontal company at which everyone shows up to work, no one tells them what to do, and all the works gets done. This model is called directed anarchy, and it's the best way to ensure creativity and innovation will flourish.

Most early-stage companies create this situation automatically. When you have only a few employees, you also have few rules and fewer naysayers. Many good companies try to keep that flatness as they grow, Google being a good example. At Google, you have your regular day job, but you are also allowed to spend 20 percent of your time doing whatever you want on your own. This policy enables at least a degree of directed anarchy. Even Steve Jobs let his people do a lot more than most people believe in terms of exploring various facets of their job independently.

Another example is Brisbane, California-based Ning.com, which creates custom social networks for its clients. At Ning, new employees and the executive team work together without any regard for titles or authority; furthermore, the company has a no-limit vacation policy—i.e., employees can take off as many weeks as they wish, provided they get their work done.

Jason Fried, the co-founder of Chicago's 37signals.com, which makes web-based applications for small businesses, designed a company with a flat organization that encourages its employees to explore horizontal connections with their co-workers and learn from their relationships. Teams are given freedom to make changes to their projects, and team members lead those projects on a rotating basis. The company also tries to avoid the traditional hierarchy by hiring "craftspeople" rather than manager types.

Similarly, the leaders of the Wisconsin architecture and design firm Kahler Slater work next to its employees in an open-layout office, which the employees had a hand in redesigning. The two co-executive officers also hold open-ended discussions with employees twice a week; the company was named one of *Entrepreneur* magazine's Best Small Businesses to Work for in 2011.

One of the best reasons to keep your company horizontal is that creative leaps do not always originate with your top players. Good ideas can come from assistants, janitors, part-time workers—people who are invisible in a strictly vertical company. When your company establishes that anyone can and should contribute, you will end up hearing some very good suggestions coming from unlikely places.

Froggy and Ilya Garcia were a husband-and-wife team in their seventies who worked on the Atari factory assembly line (staffed mostly by twenty-year-olds). As often as possible, I'd walk out to the production area and chat with the workers, trying to find out what was really going on. One day Froggy and Ilya told me that if we standardized certain components, we could build our product much faster. Once they explained how this would work, the solution was quite obvious to everyone. But no one else had noticed it. By implementing the Garcias' changes, we probably ended up saving forty dollars a machine.

INTRODUCTION
MAKE YOUR WORKPLACE AN ADVERTISEMENT
FOR YOUR COMPANY ADOPT FLEXIBLE PONGS
ADVERTISE CREATIVELY HIRE FOR PASSION
AND INTENSITY IGNORE CREDENTIALS LOOK
FOR HOBBIES USE EMPLOYEES AS RESOURCES
AVOID THE CLONES HIRE THE OBNOXIOUS HIRE
THE CRAZY FIND THE BULLIED LOOK FOR THE
LURKERS ASK ABOUT BOOKS SAIL A BOAT HIRE
UNDER YOUR NOSE COMB THROUGH TWEETS
VISIT CREATIVE COMMUNITIES BEWARE OF
POSEURS ASK ODD QUESTIONS CONDUCT DEEP
INTERVIEWS CELEBRATE INSTITUTE A DEGREE OF
ANARCHY **PROMOTE PRANKSTERISM** *SKUNK IT*
UP FOSTER FAIRNESS ISOLATE CHAMPION THE
BAD IDEAS CELEBRATE FAILURE REQUIRE RISK
REWARD TURKEYS MENTOR TREAT EMPLOYEES
AS ADULTS CREATE A CREATIVE CHAIN CREATE
A CREATIVE SPACE DESIGNATE A DEMO DAY
ENCOURAGE ADHD PRELOAD LEARN TO
TALK CREATIVE THINK TOYS NEUTRALIZE THE
NAYSAYERS WRITE DOWN OBJECTIONS TAKE
CREATIVES TO CREATIVE PLACES MAKE SOMETHING
FOR THE RICH CHANGE EVERY DAY, EVERY
HOUR THROW THE DICE DUCK PROCESSES
TAKE A RANDOM WALK THROUGH WIKIPEDIA
DON'T COUNT ON ACCOUNTING INVENT
HAPHAZARD HOLIDAYS MIX IT UP GO TO SLEEP
CONCLUSION

23

Way back in the late twentieth century, airports used to have big display ads under which sat multiple buttons. If you pushed one, you were immediately connected to some kind of service, say, a motel or a car-rental company. Late one night, Steve Wozniak decided to have some fun: He drove to the San Francisco airport and reprogrammed some of these services, switching out the companies' phone numbers with those of his friends. In the middle of the night, Steve's buddies started getting phone calls from people with questions such as "Do you have anything in midsize?" and "How much do you charge for a room?"

Steve Jobs was also something of a phone prankster, although one of his favorite tricks was more practical. He (with Wozniak) would engineer so-called blue boxes that could emulate the series of tones the telephone company used to code long-distance calls, making it possible for him to call anywhere he wanted in Europe for free. (Remember, at the time, transatlantic calls were quite expensive.) If you look at the spectrum of rule followers and rule breakers, socially acceptable rule breaking is irreverent, creative, and good-natured. Socially unacceptable rule breaking is not. You don't want to hire felons; companies that recruit from prisons don't do well. But good pranks are fun, distracting, make people laugh, and if they're really inventive, they expose someone's folly and help correct it.

A friend told me a story about a smart journalist who wrote

a successful book a few years ago and started taking himself far too seriously. So his friends at the newspaper where he worked devised an ingenious prank: They fooled him into thinking he was being interviewed for a radio program and called him, asking all kinds of ridiculous and pretentious questions—to which he responded with all kinds of ridiculous and pretentious answers. The journalist then received the tape in the mail. No one said anything further, but his arrogance level dropped immediately.

One of my favorite pranks from the Atari days happened to a guy who constantly talked about his golf game. So one day his friends replaced all the furniture in his office with actual sod and a golf pole. When he opened the door to his office the next morning, all he saw was a putting green. He significantly curtailed talk of his golf prowess.

Humor is necessary in the workplace, and pranks help people learn to laugh at themselves. People who are pompous and pretentious are not risk takers; they are not as creative. A prankster culture loosens up employees. Groupon, the Chicago-based, six-billion-dollar online social-coupon company, has a notorious prankster in its CEO and co-founder, Andrew Mason. Mason has been known to pull a wide variety of pranks, such as giving office space to a nonexistent person. He also reportedly hired a performance artist to gallivant around the company's Chicago offices in a tutu.

Online shoe retailer Zappos has created a culture where pranks are not only accepted, but also celebrated. One of the company's ten core values is to "Create fun and a little weirdness."

Think of pranks as a dress rehearsal for creativity on the job.

Caveat: Don't go too far.

INTRODUCTION MAKE YOUR WORKPLACE AN ADVERTISEMENT FOR YOUR COMPANY ADOPT FLEXIBLE PONGS ADVERTISE CREATIVELY HIRE FOR PASSION AND INTENSITY IGNORE CREDENTIALS LOOK FOR HOBBIES USE EMPLOYEES AS RESOURCES AVOID THE CLONES HIRE THE OBNOXIOUS HIRE THE CRAZY FIND THE BULLIED LOOK FOR THE LURKERS ASK ABOUT BOOKS SAIL A BOAT HIRE UNDER YOUR NOSE COMB THROUGH TWEETS VISIT CREATIVE COMMUNITIES BEWARE OF POSEURS ASK ODD QUESTIONS CONDUCT DEEP INTERVIEWS CELEBRATE INSTITUTE A DEGREE OF ANARCHY PROMOTE PRANKSTERISM **SKUNK IT UP** FOSTER FAIRNESS ISOLATE CHAMPION THE BAD IDEAS CELEBRATE FAILURE REQUIRE RISK REWARD TURKEYS MENTOR TREAT EMPLOYEES AS ADULTS CREATE A CREATIVE CHAIN CREATE A CREATIVE SPACE DESIGNATE A DEMO DAY ENCOURAGE ADHD PRELOAD LEARN TO TALK CREATIVE THINK TOYS NEUTRALIZE THE NAYSAYERS WRITE DOWN OBJECTIONS TAKE CREATIVES TO CREATIVE PLACES MAKE SOMETHING FOR THE RICH · CHANGE EVERY DAY, EVERY HOUR THROW THE DICE DUCK PROCESSES TAKE A RANDOM WALK THROUGH WIKIPEDIA DON'T COUNT ON ACCOUNTING INVENT HAPHAZARD HOLIDAYS MIX IT UP GO TO SLEEP CONCLUSION

24

As companies grow, they also tend to balloon in terms of paperwork, logistics, and hierarchies. At the same time, they tend to shrink in creativity and originality. Generally speaking, when a company reaches about 150 employees, sclerosis sets in. Once there are too many people for everyone to know each other's names, what they do, and how they do it best, the calcification intensifies. Pennies start being watched, speed to market slows down, entrepreneurship disappears, and soon your organization is basically just another big company.

One good manner of avoiding such rigidity is to branch off. This doesn't mean creating a subsidiary. Instead, create a subsidiary location. Rent another site and let people work there, away from the bureaucracy, away from the stagnation. All you need to do is water them a little, let them take root, and watch them grow their own culture.

In the 1940s, aerospace company Lockheed created a special branch and called it Skunk Works. It was enormously successful, and the name stuck. Today the term describes any group within an organization that is given a high degree of autonomy and whose mission is to work on advanced or secret projects. Sometimes companies give it a different name: Google's skunkworks is called Google X. At Google X, employees are working on special projects such as driverless cars and space elevators—although the precise nature of what Google X is doing is kept so confidential that most

Google employees themselves don't even know. Similarly, now that the company has bought Motorola, it is planning to create an Advanced Technology and Projects Division within the company; this division will convene a small group of experts to develop new technologies that can be included in Motorola's devices.

Many other companies have similar setups: Two decades ago, Microsoft established a skunkworks called Microsoft Research, to advance the state of the art in computing through basic and applied research. Likewise Ford recently created a skunkworks operation comprising eighty-five team members to redesign the company's Lincoln luxury-brand autos.

Atari had its own skunkworks as well. Located in an unused World War II-era hospital in Grass Valley, California, the place had thick walls, a bizarre floor plan, and an emergency generator in the basement. The building sat on a slight hill surrounded by pine trees, and many of us considered it one of the most beautiful spots in the world.

At Grass Valley, we assigned a core group of engineers with unique skills in electronics or mechanics to special teams. Wildly creative people, these individuals had been withering at our headquarters. Out on their own, their imagination soon broke free. A significant number of Atari's best products were spawned here, including the driving games that represented a strong profit stream for Atari. We also created the core design for the Atari 2600, a multibillion-dollar product that launched the home game-console business.

How far from your central office should you locate your skunkworks? That depends on how far out in time you want to focus. If you're looking to create projects that should soon see the light of day, your skunkworks can be as close as a block away. Your creatives can walk to it, but it's not in your face. If the projects are further down the time line, the skunkworks should be farther away. Ours was a two-hour car ride from headquarters—I didn't need to check on it on a regular basis, because the creatives were focused on projects that were a year or more off.

One of the other advantages of keeping your skunkworks at a distance is that you can relax the rules. Maybe your company doesn't allow people to sleep over. Here they can. Maybe it doesn't allow dogs. Here they're welcome. Maybe there's a dress code at the home office. Here people can wear anything they want that won't get them arrested.

Furthermore, at the main building, you need to maintain such bothersome things as guards and badges and structure. These strictures hamper creativity. You don't need them at your skunkworks.

The relative isolation of skunkworks also gives people an opportunity to hide from the daily tornado at headquarters. Most companies have a major moneymaker, a key product or service that can suck up most of the available labor. And at most places, this moneymaker is usually in some kind of crisis. As a result, the natural tendency is to pull in as many resources as possible to resolve the emergency, because the moneymaker is core to the business.

Oddly, it's often hard for many people to understand that the future is also core to the business. Businesses tend to suffer from the tyranny of now. People think now trumps later. But if there is no later, now won't do you much good. That's why you don't want creative projects to get sucked into that day-to-day morass. If all of your people—including the most creative ones—are fighting internal battles, nothing else happens.

Mind you, remoteness is becoming harder to achieve today, no thanks to Skype, texting, tweeting and so on. So you have to cloister your skunkworks not only from the emergencies but also from the trivialities of everyday life. If this means forbidding electronic communication, gulp and try it.

INTRODUCTION MAKE YOUR WORKPLACE AN ADVERTISEMENT FOR YOUR COMPANY ADOPT FLEXIBLE PONGS ADVERTISE CREATIVELY HIRE FOR PASSION AND INTENSITY IGNORE CREDENTIALS LOOK FOR HOBBIES USE EMPLOYEES AS RESOURCES AVOID THE CLONES HIRE THE OBNOXIOUS HIRE THE CRAZY FIND THE BULLIED LOOK FOR THE LURKERS ASK ABOUT BOOKS SAIL A BOAT HIRE UNDER YOUR NOSE COMB THROUGH TWEETS VISIT CREATIVE COMMUNITIES BEWARE OF POSEURS ASK ODD QUESTIONS CONDUCT DEEP INTERVIEWS CELEBRATE INSTITUTE A DEGREE OF ANARCHY PROMOTE PRANKSTERISM SKUNK IT UP **FOSTER FAIRNESS** ISOLATE CHAMPION THE BAD IDEAS CELEBRATE FAILURE REQUIRE RISK REWARD TURKEYS MENTOR TREAT EMPLOYEES AS ADULTS CREATE A CREATIVE CHAIN CREATE A CREATIVE SPACE DESIGNATE A DEMO DAY ENCOURAGE ADHD PRELOAD LEARN TO TALK CREATIVE THINK TOYS NEUTRALIZE THE NAYSAYERS WRITE DOWN OBJECTIONS TAKE CREATIVESTOCREATIVEPLACESMAKESOMETHING FOR THE RICH CHANGE EVERY DAY, EVERY HOUR THROW THE DICE DUCK PROCESSES TAKE A RANDOM WALK THROUGH WIKIPEDIA DON'T COUNT ON ACCOUNTING INVENT HAPHAZARD HOLIDAYS MIX IT UP GO TO SLEEP CONCLUSION

25

A lot of people believe they can game any system—i.e., they can figure out how to get credit for actions that weren't directly linked to positive outcomes.

Gaming a system is death to a meritocracy because the people who are gaming it destroy all semblance of fairness. And gamers are usually pretty blatant about their gaming, which tends to anger everyone else around them.

In the long run, it's best to prevent any one person from taking the credit for a new innovation or idea. At Atari, whenever a good idea began to take form on its way to reality, we would try to associate it with as many of the people as possible who helped bring it into the light. This policy created fairness, and fairness works.

Seldom is one concept ever imagined, presented, executed, and realized by a single individual. Very few good ideas coming from one person are even fully formed. Scores of decisions still have to be made, starting with developing the initial idea and culminating in the debut of the product or service. Each of these decisions is made by someone who may well be making an important, if not always highly visible, addition to the original idea.

Furthermore, if the original creator takes too much ownership of his idea, he may well try to exert too much control over it (after all, he says, it's his, and he thought of it first). Let's say he's the one who first thought up the Amazing Widget 450. If given free rein, he may become the arbiter of everything that happens to the Amazing Widget 450: its benefits, improvements, and changes.

Too much clout! No company should ever empower the person who originated the idea with the ability to censor the person making improvements, even if the product is as amazing as the Amazing Widget 450. An excellent product or service is far more likely to be the amalgam of many small improvements and ideas rather than one sudden thunderbolt.

The other problem with the credit game is that if someone is able to take all of it, you've created a culture of individual ownership. Why give the next great idea to your team when you can take it out on your own and get all the glory?

A good corporate culture allows the corporation's identity to meld with the individual employee's. Apple has created an environment where its retail employees are willing to work for relatively low wages, while creating typical sales of approximately $750,000 in three months' time. Approximately thirty thousand of Apple's 43,000 employees work in Apple retail stores for about $25,000 a year, and according to most sources, they love their work. This kind of loyalty can verge on the patriotic.

You want your company's services or products to be known as those of your company, rather than tagged to a specific creative employee. The more these ideas stay in the family, the more prosperous, and happy, everyone in the family becomes.

I N T R O D U C T I O N ·
MAKE YOUR WORKPLACE AN ADVERTISEMENT
FOR YOUR COMPANY ADOPT FLEXIBLE PONGS
ADVERTISE CREATIVELY HIRE FOR PASSION
AND INTENSITY IGNORE CREDENTIALS LOOK
FOR HOBBIES USE EMPLOYEES AS RESOURCES
AVOID THE CLONES HIRE THE OBNOXIOUS HIRE
THE CRAZY FIND THE BULLIED LOOK FOR THE
LURKERS ASK ABOUT BOOKS SAIL A BOAT HIRE
UNDER YOUR NOSE COMB THROUGH TWEETS
VISIT CREATIVE COMMUNITIES BEWARE OF
POSEURS ASK ODD QUESTIONS CONDUCT DEEP
INTERVIEWS CELEBRATE INSTITUTE A DEGREE OF
ANARCHY PROMOTE PRANKSTERISM SKUNK IT
UP FOSTER FAIRNESS **ISOLATE** CHAMPION THE
BAD IDEAS CELEBRATE FAILURE REQUIRE RISK
REWARD TURKEYS MENTOR TREAT EMPLOYEES
AS ADULTS CREATE A CREATIVE CHAIN CREATE
A CREATIVE SPACE DESIGNATE A DEMO DAY
ENCOURAGE ADHD PRELOAD LEARN TO
TALK CREATIVE THINK TOYS NEUTRALIZE THE
NAYSAYERS WRITE DOWN OBJECTIONS TAKE
CREATIVESTOCREATIVEPLACESMAKESOMETHING
FOR THE RICH CHANGE EVERY DAY, EVERY
HOUR THROW THE DICE DUCK PROCESSES
TAKE A RANDOM WALK THROUGH WIKIPEDIA
DON'T COUNT ON ACCOUNTING INVENT
HAPHAZARD HOLIDAYS MIX IT UP GO TO SLEEP
C O N C L U S I O N

26

Pajaro Dunes is a spit of sand on Monterey Bay, about twenty miles south of Santa Cruz, California, a beautiful place dotted with strange scrub trees and architecturally interesting beach houses all connected by boardwalks. At Atari, we found it was a perfect spot to hold our creative sessions, even though it was about a hundred miles from our headquarters.

Once there, we would eat, drink, smoke, and play games. And, of course, we'd talk about the business. We'd start with an overview of the state of the industry, and then discuss whatever knowledge people had to share about trade shows, potentially competitive products, distributors, and so on. Then we would talk about potential projects.

What made Pajaro effective wasn't its beauty—proximity to the ocean, amazing sunsets (although all that helped)—it was that once you were there, there was no place else to go. Unlike a hotel or a conference center, where people can wander off and do whatever they want when their meetings end, at Pajaro we relied on each other for downtime activities.

That's how you build a team: through communication—even if you have to force it. A healthy company always engenders communication between employees. One of the best ways to promote communication is to force employees to spend time together, whether they want to or not.

People who wouldn't normally listen to others do so when they're stuck together. People who wouldn't normally even talk to

113

each other do so when they're stuck together. Interesting conversations take place when you have no one else to talk to.

Furthermore, these retreats were filled with various mandatory group activities, during which we discovered that playing games such as *Risk* and *Diplomacy* could be like wearing costumes (see pong 21). We allowed ourselves to step out of our normal routines and say and feel things in front of others that we might not have felt free to say before.

We also found that, after about three days of isolation, we wore each other down. Almost anyone can maintain a façade for an hour in a conference room, but few people can do that for three days in a different and isolated environment. The mask falls off and you discover who people really are. Employees actually talk to one another, communicate better overall, and work as a team more efficiently and creatively when they are comfortable with each other.

If you're not sure how to hold a retreat, an entire industry that takes teams of employees to odd or adventurous places has sprung up to help you. Isolate and prosper!

Individual isolation

Isolation isn't just good for the soul of the group, it's good for the individual soul as well. Personally, I always need to retreat to my man cave a certain number of hours a week. The more time I spend there, the more creative I am. Steve Jobs was also a big believer in seclusion—he always told me that solitary meditation was his only path to feeling grounded. In fact, later in life he told me that he attributed his health issues to what he called the quagmire of problems he found at Apple when he returned to the company in 1997—he no longer had the time to retreat from the world.

Steve had always enjoyed meditating. In fact, he went to India in the mid-1970s to do just that. Atari paid for the trip. He had told us he was going to resign before leaving, but because we had a company problem in Europe, we told him that if he went there and fixed it, we'd pay his way, and he could come back via India.

While in India, Steve picked up a blood-related disease, returned ill, and then rejoined Atari, where he and Steve Wozniak became the engineers of record for our very successful *Breakout* game—a project that no other engineer had wanted to work on because it was a ball-and-paddle game. After the passion for *Pong* and its ilk had faded, the market for such games had dried up. But the Steves saw potential where no one else could.

Steve was always a fan of keeping life simple and meditative. Case in point: Usually he would visit me, but once in the 1980s when I was out riding my motorcycle, I decided to drop in on him and see the house he'd bought a year before. I knocked on the door and it took him a long time to answer—I'd woken him up, although it was well after noon. He proceeded to ask me into a home that looked as though he had just moved in—there was almost no furniture, and almost no food, just some tea and fruit. We then sat under a tree on a bench in the backyard, where he told me that this house represented what he'd always wanted in life: as little clutter as possible.

I strongly believe that everyone who wants to be creative must find a place where his or her mind can be alone and untouched by the insanity of complexity. There is a place, a state of mind, somewhere between cognitive reasoning and dreaming, a place you can find just before you go to sleep or just after you wake up. It is from here that imaginative thoughts spring.

INTRODUCTION MAKE YOUR WORKPLACE AN ADVERTISEMENT FOR YOUR COMPANY ADOPT FLEXIBLE PONGS ADVERTISE CREATIVELY HIRE FOR PASSION AND INTENSITY IGNORE CREDENTIALS LOOK FOR HOBBIES USE EMPLOYEES AS RESOURCES AVOID THE CLONES HIRE THE OBNOXIOUS HIRE THE CRAZY FIND THE BULLIED LOOK FOR THE LURKERS ASK ABOUT BOOKS SAIL A BOAT HIRE UNDER YOUR NOSE COMB THROUGH TWEETS VISIT CREATIVE COMMUNITIES BEWARE OF POSEURS ASK ODD QUESTIONS CONDUCT DEEP INTERVIEWS CELEBRATE INSTITUTE A DEGREE OF ANARCHY PROMOTE PRANKSTERISM SKUNK IT UP FOSTER FAIRNESS ISOLATE **CHAMPION THE BAD IDEAS** CELEBRATE FAILURE REQUIRE RISK REWARD TURKEYS MENTOR TREAT EMPLOYEES AS ADULTS CREATE A CREATIVE CHAIN CREATE A CREATIVE SPACE DESIGNATE A DEMO DAY ENCOURAGE ADHD PRELOAD LEARN TO TALK CREATIVE THINK TOYS NEUTRALIZE THE NAYSAYERS WRITE DOWN OBJECTIONS TAKE CREATIVESTOCREATIVEPLACESMAKESOMETHING FOR THE RICH CHANGE EVERY DAY, EVERY HOUR THROW THE DICE DUCK PROCESSES TAKE A RANDOM WALK THROUGH WIKIPEDIA DON'T COUNT ON ACCOUNTING INVENT HAPHAZARD HOLIDAYS MIX IT UP GO TO SLEEP CONCLUSION

27

At Pajaro Dunes, I used to employ one of my favorite tricks for enhancing creativity: I would ask everyone to make a list of all the ideas that had been presented at our meetings, and then have them rank those ideas from good to bad. I would then take the six items on the bottom of the list and say, "Let's suppose we were restricted for the next few months to work just on these six terrible projects. How do we make them work?"

This process reversed people's normal mental dynamic. Instead of trying to figure out what's wrong with something, which triggers people's critical instincts, here they had to figure out what was right with something, which triggers people's creative instincts.

Every time we did this exercise, at least one of the bottom six ideas turned out to be not just good, but great, and eventually became a profit-making machine for us. The best was a gun game called *Quack*, in which players shot guns at ducks. At first the idea sounded dreadful, but once we figured out how to make the gun work in a really clever way, the game became enormously successful.

I adapted this particular technique from my high school debating coach, who told us on our first day of practice that we were going to have to learn to debate both sides of any proposition. We all soon discovered that arguing for something you don't believe can turn your understanding of the world upside down, and help you to see issues you had not been able to see before.

One of the problems with today's educational system is that it often turns the most creative people into the least creative. Over and over, the process teaches kids to self-edit, to conform, to blend in. If the picture Jennie drew of a flower doesn't look exactly like the teacher's concept of a flower, then Jennie drew a bad picture. Eventually Jennie learns to say, "This isn't what they want me to do, so I better conform or I'll get bad grades."

The goal for a successful company is to do the opposite: Encourage the odd, the unusual, the remarkable. It might be the biggest driver of success your company will ever know.

INTRODUCTION MAKE YOUR WORKPLACE AN ADVERTISEMENT FOR YOUR COMPANY ADOPT FLEXIBLE PONGS ADVERTISE CREATIVELY HIRE FOR PASSION AND INTENSITY IGNORE CREDENTIALS LOOK FOR HOBBIES USE EMPLOYEES AS RESOURCES AVOID THE CLONES HIRE THE OBNOXIOUS HIRE THE CRAZY FIND THE BULLIED LOOK FOR THE LURKERS ASK ABOUT BOOKS SAIL A BOAT HIRE UNDER YOUR NOSE COMB THROUGH TWEETS VISIT CREATIVE COMMUNITIES BEWARE OF POSEURS ASK ODD QUESTIONS CONDUCT DEEP INTERVIEWS CELEBRATE INSTITUTE A DEGREE OF ANARCHY PROMOTE PRANKSTERISM SKUNK IT UP FOSTER FAIRNESS ISOLATE CHAMPION THE BAD IDEAS **CELEBRATE FAILURE** *REQUIRE RISK REWARD TURKEYS MENTOR TREAT EMPLOYEES AS ADULTS CREATE A CREATIVE CHAIN CREATE A CREATIVE SPACE DESIGNATE A DEMO DAY ENCOURAGE ADHD PRELOAD LEARN TO TALK CREATIVE THINK TOYS NEUTRALIZE THE NAYSAYERS WRITE DOWN OBJECTIONS TAKE CREATIVES TO CREATIVE PLACES MAKE SOMETHING FOR THE RICH CHANGE EVERY DAY, EVERY HOUR THROW THE DICE DUCK PROCESSES TAKE A RANDOM WALK THROUGH WIKIPEDIA DON'T COUNT ON ACCOUNTING INVENT HAPHAZARD HOLIDAYS MIX IT UP GO TO SLEEP CONCLUSION*

28

If people are reluctant to suggest bad ideas, they are absolutely terrified of failure. And if they're terrified of failure, they likely won't succeed. Your company must make failure a tenable option.

Of course, you never actually plan for failure. But failure happens whenever you try something new. It must. If you're learning to ski and you never fall down, you never get better. You must take new risks to learn new skills. You have to fail to succeed. Failure is an important teacher.

Furthermore, failures are almost never total. You must look at all aspects of a project to see whether it is really as much of a disaster as you first feared. The truth is that if you're paying attention, you can learn a great deal from failure. People who are afraid of failure—and afraid of talking about it—will miss out on all the excellent data that results from trying something new and different.

For example, Apple's early 1980s computer model, the Lisa, was a fiasco. Lisa was slow and expensive. Few people liked it. It didn't sell. But a great deal of what Apple learned through Lisa's failure showed up in its next model, the Mac, which was a huge success. The company wouldn't have been able to figure out how to make the Mac so good if the Lisa hadn't been so bad.

Likewise, the first Chuck E. Cheese's was a flop. We gambled that 5,000 square feet would be enough space for our restaurant, but on opening day we realized that we'd made a terrible mistake. The space was far too small. What an unpleasant situation: Everyone was jammed in on top of each other and the entire place was filled with noise and chaos. I was surprised anyone ever came back. But now we knew exactly what we had done wrong. Our next restaurant was 20,000 square feet—a big, cavernous, wonderful place. We would have never tried something so large for our first one because restaurants had never been that big before. But it turned out that's what we needed, and only by failing did we find this out.

Furthermore, by accepting failure as a necessary part of your business, you rid your employees of the constant fear that if they do something—anything—wrong, they'll be canned. Fear of failure creates an organization that says no to every new idea. That organization will be saying no until the day it closes its doors with a final no: "No Longer in Business."

The history of business is filled with companies that almost failed, but used those failures to successfully reinvent themselves. For example, in the 1990s the SEGA Corp. competed fiercely with Nintendo and Sony for domination in the video-game console market. When the SEGA Dreamcast console failed, the company was on the brink of collapse. SEGA decided to restructure and, in 2001, chose to drop making consoles altogether. By focusing on publishing games from its recognizable brands on other consoles as well as by acquiring smaller game-making companies, SEGA was back on track by 2005.

One of my favorite failure stories is that of the ubiquitous household product WD-40. It's called that because the first 39 versions of the product failed; WD-40 stands for "Water displacement, 40th formula."

Certainly plenty of entrepreneurs started off as failures only to find success. Akio Morita formed a company whose first product was a rice cooker that, unfortunately, burned the rice. The company went on to success in other areas—it's now Sony. Henry Ford's first two automobile companies failed, but that didn't stop him from founding the Ford Motor Company.

Even people in the middle of great success can have great failures and learn from them: We all know Sir Richard Branson's Virgin Records and Virgin Airlines, but how many remember Virgin Cola or Virgin Vodka?

Of course, there's a right way and a wrong way to fail. Failure is useful, but too many failures can cause you to fail for good. Unless you're going for broke, and have good reason to do it, never bet more than a small portion of your assets on any one idea. That way, the project can be a total failure and yet allow you not just to survive but also to learn a great deal of valuable information.

I N T R O D U C T I O N
MAKE YOUR WORKPLACE AN ADVERTISEMENT
FOR YOUR COMPANY ADOPT FLEXIBLE PONGS
ADVERTISE CREATIVELY HIRE FOR PASSION
AND INTENSITY IGNORE CREDENTIALS LOOK
FOR HOBBIES USE EMPLOYEES AS RESOURCES
AVOID THE CLONES HIRE THE OBNOXIOUS HIRE
THE CRAZY FIND THE BULLIED LOOK FOR THE
LURKERS ASK ABOUT BOOKS SAIL A BOAT HIRE
UNDER YOUR NOSE COMB THROUGH TWEETS
VISIT CREATIVE COMMUNITIES BEWARE OF
POSEURS ASK ODD QUESTIONS CONDUCT DEEP
INTERVIEWS CELEBRATE INSTITUTE A DEGREE OF
ANARCHY PROMOTE PRANKSTERISM SKUNK IT
UP FOSTER FAIRNESS ISOLATE CHAMPION THE
BAD IDEAS CELEBRATE FAILURE **REQUIRE RISK**
REWARD TURKEYS MENTOR TREAT EMPLOYEES
AS ADULTS CREATE A CREATIVE CHAIN CREATE
A CREATIVE SPACE DESIGNATE A DEMO DAY
ENCOURAGE ADHD PRELOAD LEARN TO
TALK CREATIVE THINK TOYS NEUTRALIZE THE
NAYSAYERS WRITE DOWN OBJECTIONS TAKE
CREATIVESTOCREATIVEPLACESMAKESOMETHING
FOR THE RICH CHANGE EVERY DAY, EVERY
HOUR THROW THE DICE DUCK PROCESSES
TAKE A RANDOM WALK THROUGH WIKIPEDIA
DON'T COUNT ON ACCOUNTING INVENT
HAPHAZARD HOLIDAYS MIX IT UP GO TO SLEEP
C O N C L U S I O N

29

Everyone knows that risks are necessary. Many of the greatest advances in science, exploration, medicine, and business would never have occurred if someone hadn't been willing to walk— literally or metaphorically—into uncharted territory. Think of the Wright brothers, flying into the air for the first time; civil rights hero Rosa Parks, sitting down in the white section of a bus; Renaissance scientist Galileo Galilei, risking death to disobey Catholic Church prohibitions and become the father of modern astronomy; or Indian leader Mahatma Gandhi, also risking death to lead nonviolent resistance in the fight for independence.

Many companies today have survived only because their founders were willing to take risks. Take, for example, the on-line music service Pandora: In 2001, its owners were out of money and decided to risk everything on the company's future, meaning that more than fifty employees deferred their salaries for two years and founder Tim Westergren maxed out eleven credit cards until the company was rescued by an eight-million-dollar venture-capital investment in 2004. Today, the company is worth $1.58 billion. Then there's Sir James Dyson, the founder of Dyson Ltd., who so believed in his ability to create a great vacuum cleaner that he made more than 5,000 prototypes and went four million dollars into debt. In 2011, the company made one billion dollars, and Dyson's net worth was reportedly more than two billion dollars.

Still, despite the fact that we all tell each other stories about how great successes were made possible by great risks, risk terrifies most people. Why? Because they dread uncertainty and failure. Risk opens the door to both of these possibilities.

The very definition of risk involves an uncertain future outcome. This does not make the human brain happy. The brain wants to predict the future accurately. The surer we are about our environment, the safer we feel. It's been that way for eons. What kind of crops are we going to grow, what strengths do our enemies possess, what's the weather going to be like, is that saber-toothed tiger over there going to eat us?

Today we don't take many life-or-death risks, but we do take some that could mean life or death for our business—and people tend to be afraid of them.

Yet one of the best ways a company can create a healthy ecosystem that fertilizes creativity is to include risk. That doesn't mean doing anything silly or poorly planned. Risks can be smart, or foolish, or anything in between. But all companies should have a budget that allows them to spend a certain amount or percentage on projects that are not guaranteed to succeed, and on ideas that allow creatives to figure out solutions to problems that others might not yet see as such.

Of course, at some businesses—particularly small ones—risk is the only possibility they know. At Atari, our entire business model was based on risk. Our competition was bigger, stronger, and better at marketing, so we were forced to rely on our culture of creativity to survive. The fish is the last guy to understand water. We were fish. It was all we knew.

Today, with the business environment changing so quickly, companies have to be innovative to survive—even if that means changing their risk-averse culture. And certainly hiring a Steve

Jobs is part of that change. The truth is that very few companies would hire Steve, even today. Why? Because he was an outlier. To most potential employers, he'd just seem like a jerk in bad clothing. And yet a jerk in bad clothing can be exactly the right guy to give your company the highest market capitalization in the world.

Taking a risk shouldn't be considered an option in the twenty-first century. It is a necessity. Yet too many companies have become so risk-averse that when quick, decisive, powerful action becomes imperative, they can't take it. And that is the primary reason why companies must allow their creatives to take risks—today's business environment changes so rapidly that at any moment another company can come along and take away your customers. A risky move is generally necessary to fight back. But if your company doesn't have a culture of risk-taking, you won't know how to do it when the need arises—and it will.

Simply put, risk taking is compulsory because it is the best way to ensure a successful future.

However, do not forget that risk is risky. I learned this lesson the hard way. Back in 1984, I wanted to create a little robot that would be a combination friend, servant, and pet—a mechanical creature that could chat pleasantly, fetch things, and help manage your day. Who wouldn't want a sweet little metal buddy to make life a little more organized and a little less lonely?

Convinced this was a brilliant idea, I put in all the cash I could come up with: $14 million. But the robot didn't quite work. Everything was in place, yet there was one problem. As the little guy roamed around the house, he'd pick up static electricity and his computer would crash. Now, if your PC crashes, you get the blue screen of death. It can make you crazy. But that's all. If a forty-pound robot crashes, it can tumble down a staircase and kill someone. A blue screen of death is preferable to actual death. We called this problem the "mow down the baby mode." It was not a good thing.

Try as we might, we couldn't find a way to insulate the robot's computer to keep it immune from electronic static. Eventually the company failed, and although I was able to sell some of its technology to Kodak, it was pretty much a total loss.

This was the first time I'd ever felt intimidated by technical issues. I had been most concerned about marketing and pricing issues; it had never occurred to me that I wouldn't be able to solve something technical. I was technically very arrogant. Not any longer.

More important, I learned that you don't put all your risk eggs in one basket. From then on, I declared, my company would never risk more than 10 percent of our engineering budget on the weird or the different. While you must keep taking risks, you have to be reasonable about how much of your resources you allot to them.

And you need to be specific. This is how most people talk about risk:

"How much could we lose on the project?"

"A lot."

"How much more than we can *afford* to lose?"

"A lot."

"What could this risk cost us in the long run?"

"It could cost a whole lot."

This dialogue is not helpful. You want an exchange that's more like this:

"If this project goes belly up, what could we lose?"

"Twenty thousand dollars."

It's much easier to face your fears about risk when you've done your best to quantify it. Make it real. Then you can walk away without the sense that one failure could doom everything. The more you can understand the risks you are taking, and the better you can quantify them in terms of cash to be earned or lost, the more likely you are to make a sound decision. Abstract talk amplifies the fear of risk. Concrete talk diminishes it.

Face your fear with data.

you set to quantify it. Make it real. Then you can walk away

INTRODUCTION
MAKE YOUR WORKPLACE AN ADVERTISEMENT
FOR YOUR COMPANY ADOPT FLEXIBLE PONGS
ADVERTISE CREATIVELY HIRE FOR PASSION
AND INTENSITY IGNORE CREDENTIALS LOOK
FOR HOBBIES USE EMPLOYEES AS RESOURCES
AVOID THE CLONES HIRE THE OBNOXIOUS HIRE
THE CRAZY FIND THE BULLIED LOOK FOR THE
LURKERS ASK ABOUT BOOKS SAIL A BOAT HIRE
UNDER YOUR NOSE COMB THROUGH TWEETS
VISIT CREATIVE COMMUNITIES BEWARE OF
POSEURS ASK ODD QUESTIONS CONDUCT DEEP
INTERVIEWS CELEBRATE INSTITUTE A DEGREE OF
ANARCHY PROMOTE PRANKSTERISM SKUNK IT
UP FOSTER FAIRNESS ISOLATE CHAMPION THE
BAD IDEAS CELEBRATE FAILURE REQUIRE RISK
REWARD TURKEYS MENTOR TREAT EMPLOYEES
AS ADULTS CREATE A CREATIVE CHAIN CREATE
A CREATIVE SPACE DESIGNATE A DEMO DAY
ENCOURAGE ADHD PRELOAD LEARN TO
TALK CREATIVE THINK TOYS NEUTRALIZE THE
NAYSAYERS WRITE DOWN OBJECTIONS TAKE
CREATIVES TO CREATIVE PLACES MAKE SOMETHING
FOR THE RICH CHANGE EVERY DAY, EVERY
HOUR THROW THE DICE DUCK PROCESSES
TAKE A RANDOM WALK THROUGH WIKIPEDIA
DON'T COUNT ON ACCOUNTING INVENT
HAPHAZARD HOLIDAYS MIX IT UP GO TO SLEEP
CONCLUSION

30

If your company is not making mistakes once in a while, you are not pushing the envelope. I've always felt that truly bad ideas, the fascinatingly terrible ones, deserve some kind of recognition. Why not make screwing up less frightening by celebrating it?

So at Chuck E. Cheese's, we instituted what we called the Turkey Award. Four times a year, we invited our regional managers from across the country to dinners at which we would discuss the successes of the previous four months, as well as our plans for the next four. During the event we held the normal after-dinner awards ceremony, with the various normal after-dinner awards— best employee, best manager, best results, and so on. Then, however, came the one everyone was waiting for: the Turkey Award, given to the biggest screw-up of the previous four months. The award itself was something I found at a Mexican bazaar, eighteen inches of God-awful, poultry-shaped tin.

I felt that by acknowledging and laughing at the most notable failure, we would take the sting out of it. So we would accept nominations from the floor, asking people to applaud for the worst failures and using my arm as the audiometer.

The winner had to keep the ugly tin turkey on his desk for the next four months.

One award was given to our operations manager for his proposal to get customers to bus their own tables. He thought that if cleaning tables could be made so much fun that people would want to do it themselves, we could save a great deal in labor costs.

The idea was to have a giant coin slot that, when you inserted a pizza tray, would vend a token that could be used to play the games. Next to the slot would be a fiberglass character named Mr. Munch (who loved pizza) with an open mouth containing a suction fan that would suck napkins from your hand. When the napkin went into the mouth, it would burp and say, "Thank you." Everyone loved it.

That was the problem. Way too much love. When we actually implemented this idea, the kids would scan the tables for any pizza trays left unguarded. Many customers would leave food on their table when they went into the game room, only to return and find their pizza sitting on the table itself, the tray having been taken and then turned in to the machine by the kids.

Best turkey ever.

INTRODUCTION
MAKE YOUR WORKPLACE AN ADVERTISEMENT
FOR YOUR COMPANY ADOPT FLEXIBLE PONGS
ADVERTISE CREATIVELY HIRE FOR PASSION
AND INTENSITY IGNORE CREDENTIALS LOOK
FOR HOBBIES USE EMPLOYEES AS RESOURCES
AVOID THE CLONES HIRE THE OBNOXIOUS HIRE
THE CRAZY FIND THE BULLIED LOOK FOR THE
LURKERS ASK ABOUT BOOKS SAIL A BOAT HIRE
UNDER YOUR NOSE COMB THROUGH TWEETS
VISIT CREATIVE COMMUNITIES BEWARE OF
POSEURS ASK ODD QUESTIONS CONDUCT DEEP
INTERVIEWS CELEBRATE INSTITUTE A DEGREE OF
ANARCHY PROMOTE PRANKSTERISM SKUNK IT
UP FOSTER FAIRNESS ISOLATE CHAMPION THE
BAD IDEAS CELEBRATE FAILURE REQUIRE RISK
REWARD TURKEYS **MENTOR** TREAT EMPLOYEES
AS ADULTS CREATE A CREATIVE CHAIN CREATE
A CREATIVE SPACE DESIGNATE A DEMO DAY
ENCOURAGE ADHD PRELOAD LEARN TO
TALK CREATIVE THINK TOYS NEUTRALIZE THE
NAYSAYERS WRITE DOWN OBJECTIONS TAKE
CREATIVES TO CREATIVE PLACES MAKE SOMETHING
FOR THE RICH CHANGE EVERY DAY, EVERY
HOUR THROW THE DICE DUCK PROCESSES
TAKE A RANDOM WALK THROUGH WIKIPEDIA
DON'T COUNT ON ACCOUNTING INVENT
HAPHAZARD HOLIDAYS MIX IT UP GO TO SLEEP
CONCLUSION

31

Mentoring is extremely valuable—just because it's a well-worn word doesn't mean it's an overly worn concept. Mentors can serve the usual purpose of helping anyone who's young or new at a job, but in general, it's the creative people who need mentors more than others.

By definition, creatives are always working on something that's different, innovative, and new. That means most of the people around them aren't going to understand what they're doing, why they're doing it, or where they're going with it. They may have no idea what "it" even is.

This puts the creatives in an almost constant confrontational mode with the rest of the company. There they are, trying to explain their new projects to their bosses, and when these brick walls reply, "I just don't get it," that's rejection, pure and simple. It hurts. To be creative is to go through a tremendous and constant amount of rejection.

They may be incomprehensible, but these kinds of projects drive your company. Too often, however, the person driving them is being edited and managed and curbed, and projects that, if properly developed and overseen, could make your company a fortune don't even get a chance to start.

All companies must make sure that someone is supporting their creatives: someone who is reassuring, clear, and who can help them stay on track. This is the role of the mentor. She stops the creatives from feeling so rejected and lonely that their work suffers. She offers to fight the bureaucracy, even if she doesn't understand the product. She doesn't always have to understand exactly what her protégés are doing as much as be willing to fight for their right to do it. If she does her job well, the company will profit immensely. If she does it poorly, your competitors will take over your market.

Note: Out-of-company mentoring is also important. Most companies don't know how to mentor their own creatives, so if this applies to you, try to find ways to connect your creatives with possible mentors outside the company.

Steve Jobs didn't come over to my house to get ideas from me. He wanted to bounce around some of his own ideas and pick up some courage when I supported them, as odd as they might be. I often didn't completely understand these ideas, but I would tell him that he seemed to have a clear vision, and that if he could foresee a positive outcome, he should stay the course even if no one around him understood his goals.

I remember one time when Steve came over to Woodside to talk about the Unix operating environment. This was during the years after he had left Apple to found the NeXT computer. Unix was an expensive and heavy system for a minicomputer, and whether or not to use it was a difficult choice for him to make. He wasn't sure what to do.

I encouraged him to follow his instincts. Unix was clearly the best architecture at the time, but it did have issues—it was a memory and processor hog, making the machines it ran sluggish, and it also had a slow optical drive. But people were using it at scientific workstations, and Steve wanted NeXT to be halfway between a workstation and a personal computer.

Still, Unix was great in many ways, and it had this wonderful multi-threaded architecture—you could run different applications at the same time, then unheard of in a personal computer. With Unix, if one app crashed, it didn't crash the whole system.

We talked about Unix for hours, going back and forth about its advantages and disadvantages. I didn't see my role as telling Steve what to do as much as letting him hear himself argue both sides of the issue and then letting him know that I supported him totally and had absolute confidence that he would make the right decision.

Ultimately Steve decided to use Unix, and although things didn't work out perfectly, it did turn out to be the right choice at the right time. In 1996, Apple ended up buying NeXT for $429 million—and the company's next operating system was based on Unix.

I've had many great mentors. One of my best was Bob Noyce. Dubbed The Mayor of Silicon Valley, he co-founded Fairchild Semiconductor and Intel Corporation and is also co-credited with the invention of the microchip. I met Bob through an American Electronics Association dinner, and when it became clear that we both liked chess, we started playing regular games.

Bob was enormously helpful to me, especially in terms of business advice. Back then being only twenty-nine years old and running a large company was very unusual—perhaps hard to believe considering all of the high-profile young executives in business now. In fact, it was frightening. No one ever really knew how truly scared I was. My way of dealing with my fear was to fake it, which led to a great many blunders. It took me years to find out it was acceptable not to know all the answers, and to ask other people for help.

Bob helped teach me this. He gave me the confidence to believe in myself, because he believed in me. He always made me feel a little like a teenager, because he was so wise and would say very intuitive things that changed my life, both personally and in business. These profound comments were often in response to a simple question, or sometimes even just a quip he made during a conversation.

Here are two examples:

"If the other guy's business looks easy, it means you don't know enough about it." I have contemplated this idea over and over again when I think I've discovered an opportunity that is being overlooked by another business. By digging deeper, I almost always find there are obstacles that I hadn't noticed in my casual analysis.

"Examples of failed products or projects are hard to find. Successes are easy." In other words, failed products are often hidden on purpose or, because they didn't go anywhere, were never advertised or were simply not noticed by the market. In the late 1980s I had a toy company for which we would repeatedly build prototypes and then present them to Toys "R" Us buyers for their opinions. We soon became friendly with these people, and they were very enthusiastic about many of our products, yet they would say over and over, "Oh, that old thing again." They then would name a company that had tried to market the same idea, and describe how it had failed miserably in the market. Once we had the chance to discuss these product failures, it became obvious why they failed. I was always embarrassed that I had not seen it earlier.

INTRODUCTION
MAKE YOUR WORKPLACE AN ADVERTISEMENT
FOR YOUR COMPANY ADOPT FLEXIBLE PONGS
ADVERTISE CREATIVELY HIRE FOR PASSION
AND INTENSITY IGNORE CREDENTIALS LOOK
FOR HOBBIES USE EMPLOYEES AS RESOURCES
AVOID THE CLONES HIRE THE OBNOXIOUS HIRE
THE CRAZY FIND THE BULLIED LOOK FOR THE
LURKERS ASK ABOUT BOOKS SAIL A BOAT HIRE
UNDER YOUR NOSE COMB THROUGH TWEETS
VISIT CREATIVE COMMUNITIES BEWARE OF
POSEURS ASK ODD QUESTIONS CONDUCT DEEP
INTERVIEWS CELEBRATE INSTITUTE A DEGREE OF
ANARCHY PROMOTE PRANKSTERISM SKUNK IT
UP FOSTER FAIRNESS ISOLATE CHAMPION THE
BAD IDEAS CELEBRATE FAILURE REQUIRE RISK
REWARD TURKEYS MENTOR **TREAT EMPLOYEES
AS ADULTS** CREATE A CREATIVE CHAIN CREATE
A CREATIVE SPACE DESIGNATE A DEMO DAY
ENCOURAGE ADHD PRELOAD LEARN TO
TALK CREATIVE THINK TOYS NEUTRALIZE THE
NAYSAYERS WRITE DOWN OBJECTIONS TAKE
CREATIVES TO CREATIVE PLACES MAKE SOMETHING
FOR THE RICH CHANGE EVERY DAY, EVERY
HOUR THROW THE DICE DUCK PROCESSES
TAKE A RANDOM WALK THROUGH WIKIPEDIA
DON'T COUNT ON ACCOUNTING INVENT
HAPHAZARD HOLIDAYS MIX IT UP GO TO SLEEP
CONCLUSION

32

Many corporate cultures gear themselves around the concept that creatives can't really be trusted and need constant supervision. This is what I call the kindergarten school of management. It works no better than having a bunch of actual kindergarteners run the creative side of your company.

The problem is that more often than not, it's the supervisors who are the real children. At most companies, creative people are working hard to innovate and yet, instead of receiving proper encouragement, they are being disparaged by childish minds. That's why the comic strip *Dilbert* hits home so powerfully—most (or perhaps all) of us in the work force have had bosses whose intelligence level was less than stellar.

This happens too often because someone who is good at his job at a base level is eventually promoted to a position where he is out of his depth—aka the Peter Principle: Employees tend to rise to their level of incompetence.

This is why those who are tasked with making decisions tend to be the ones who least understand the ramifications of these decisions. They are not the ones who've been to the recent trade shows; they are not the ones who are constantly combing the Internet for new ideas; they are not the ones who know what's going on in the culture because they are participating in it. They are the ones whose new job as a so-called responsible manager has distanced them from the reality of the marketplace. As a result, they don't understand what the creatives are doing, and they over-supervise them, trying to rein them in instead of encouraging their imaginative juices to flow.

What is most management about? Acting as though creatives are children, and stopping them from putting their interesting, risky, and potentially valuable ideas into practice.

What should management be about? Treating creatives like adults, and helping them put their interesting, risky, and potentially valuable ideas into practice.

Note: Management has one other critical task. Creatives are often poor communicators. For example, Steve Wozniak was possibly the worst speaker I ever met—he could barely get words out of his mouth, and he addressed his feet rather than me whenever we talked. In the early days, he was clearly a hyper-creative, but without Steve Jobs no one would have known. (Woz has since become quite a skilled communicator.)

The skills that make people highly creative do not necessarily make them articulate or even glib. So the other important task of a manager is to communicate for them—to recognize the good in their project and then become their in-house public-relations director. A great manager is a great cheerleader—of adults.

I N T R O D U C T I O N
MAKE YOUR WORKPLACE AN ADVERTISEMENT
FOR YOUR COMPANY ADOPT FLEXIBLE PONGS
ADVERTISE CREATIVELY HIRE FOR PASSION
AND INTENSITY IGNORE CREDENTIALS LOOK
FOR HOBBIES USE EMPLOYEES AS RESOURCES
AVOID THE CLONES HIRE THE OBNOXIOUS HIRE
THE CRAZY FIND THE BULLIED LOOK FOR THE
LURKERS ASK ABOUT BOOKS SAIL A BOAT HIRE
UNDER YOUR NOSE COMB THROUGH TWEETS
VISIT CREATIVE COMMUNITIES BEWARE OF
POSEURS ASK ODD QUESTIONS CONDUCT DEEP
INTERVIEWS CELEBRATE INSTITUTE A DEGREE OF
ANARCHY PROMOTE PRANKSTERISM SKUNK IT
UP FOSTER FAIRNESS ISOLATE CHAMPION THE
BAD IDEAS CELEBRATE FAILURE REQUIRE RISK
REWARD TURKEYS MENTOR TREAT EMPLOYEES
AS ADULTS **CREATE A CREATIVE CHAIN** CREATE
A CREATIVE SPACE DESIGNATE A DEMO DAY
ENCOURAGE ADHD PRELOAD LEARN TO
TALK CREATIVE THINK TOYS NEUTRALIZE THE
NAYSAYERS WRITE DOWN OBJECTIONS TAKE
CREATIVES TO CREATIVE PLACES MAKE SOMETHING
FOR THE RICH CHANGE EVERY DAY, EVERY
HOUR THROW THE DICE DUCK PROCESSES
TAKE A RANDOM WALK THROUGH WIKIPEDIA
DON'T COUNT ON ACCOUNTING INVENT
HAPHAZARD HOLIDAYS MIX IT UP GO TO SLEEP
C O N C L U S I O N

33

If you ask a group of people if they are creative, nearly all of them will say they are. If you give a speech and ask everyone in the audience who believes in innovation to raise his or her hand, everyone does. But when the time comes to present your bosses with your creative, innovative idea, the odds are good no one is going to believe in you. Creative innovation is just too radical, too scary, and unfortunately, too unbelievable to most people. Terrific in the abstract. Not terrific in real life.

A lot of people, including the executives of many companies, have it in their minds that they embrace innovation, but when it comes to specifics, they become powerful naysayers. This is the opposite of a Steve Jobs. Steve was not particularly creative himself, but he was extraordinarily open to creativity, very willing to brave risks. He embraced innovation and brought it to the fore.

It's been said that creativity is the art of concealing your sources. You see something and say, "Gee, that is interesting. If it were this, or that, it would be successful." Then, if and when you help make it happen and it works, you can take some form of credit for it. You didn't come up with the idea, but you saw its potential.

The truth is that creative ideas, products or services are not produced by lightning strikes. They evolve in these gradual, step-by-step processes of analysis and solution. To allow that progression to happen, you must have in place a chain of command (ideally as short a chain as possible) that does everything it can to promote a good idea and help it see fruition rather than stifle it. If your management system is composed of many steps, and each step must first be approved, and approval must come from a doubting management, creativity will wither.

To ensure that creativity flourishes, examine if and how creative ideas bubble to the top at your company. Is there a chain of command that nurtures and promotes them? Or is there a chain that drags them down, guaranteeing they'll never see the light of day?

Companies have to ask themselves: Do we really want creatives? Some companies hire consultant after consultant to discuss creativity, but all they're doing is adding to a chain of command that halts rather than stimulates it. The idea is to create a management process that, step for step, recognizes, enhances, and executes creative ideas. If your company isn't doing that, it's not going to last.

INTRODUCTION
MAKE YOUR WORKPLACE AN ADVERTISEMENT
FOR YOUR COMPANY ADOPT FLEXIBLE PONGS
ADVERTISE CREATIVELY HIRE FOR PASSION
AND INTENSITY IGNORE CREDENTIALS LOOK
FOR HOBBIES USE EMPLOYEES AS RESOURCES
AVOID THE CLONES HIRE THE OBNOXIOUS HIRE
THE CRAZY FIND THE BULLIED LOOK FOR THE
LURKERS ASK ABOUT BOOKS SAIL A BOAT HIRE
UNDER YOUR NOSE COMB THROUGH TWEETS
VISIT CREATIVE COMMUNITIES BEWARE OF
POSEURS ASK ODD QUESTIONS CONDUCT DEEP
INTERVIEWS CELEBRATE INSTITUTE A DEGREE OF
ANARCHY PROMOTE PRANKSTERISM SKUNK IT
UP FOSTER FAIRNESS ISOLATE CHAMPION THE
BAD IDEAS CELEBRATE FAILURE REQUIRE RISK
REWARD TURKEYS MENTOR TREAT EMPLOYEES
AS ADULTS CREATE A CREATIVE CHAIN **CREATE
A CREATIVE SPACE** DESIGNATE A DEMO DAY
ENCOURAGE ADHD PRELOAD LEARN TO
TALK CREATIVE THINK TOYS NEUTRALIZE THE
NAYSAYERS WRITE DOWN OBJECTIONS TAKE
CREATIVES TO CREATIVE PLACES MAKE SOMETHING
FOR THE RICH CHANGE EVERY DAY, EVERY
HOUR THROW THE DICE DUCK PROCESSES
TAKE A RANDOM WALK THROUGH WIKIPEDIA
DON'T COUNT ON ACCOUNTING INVENT
HAPHAZARD HOLIDAYS MIX IT UP GO TO SLEEP
CONCLUSION

34

When we were looking around for real estate to start the digital entertainment company uWink (my eighteenth start-up), we eventually found the perfect building in Los Angeles: It had a lot of space, a terrific location, and an extremely low price. The only problem with the building was the building itself. It was a wreck, with many floors that had been cut up into dark little offices with stained and broken ceiling tiles and tired little light fixtures hanging down from the ceiling like sick animals. The worn carpets were filthy—to the extent they were still there—and the walls were even worse. It looked as though raves had been going on throughout and no one had ever cleaned up afterward.

We wanted to make the place livable, but we didn't want to spend a great deal of money. So we decided to paint all the walls with blackboard paint and then put up particle board panels to break up the long patches of black. About every ten feet, we placed boxes filled with chalk and erasers.

The place turned out to be a creative heaven. People would write their name on the wall outside their office, then start messing around with signing their titles. We didn't have a lot of them, and the ones we had soon morphed into the fantastically odd. One man wrote his name on the wall, drew a crown over it, and gave himself the title Lord of the Mystic Realm.

Chalk, we realized, has many benefits, but one of its greatest is its impermanence, which encourages people to be creative when writing on walls because there is no long-term risk in doing so. I could have told the staff to do whatever they wanted with paint, but paint is permanent, posing higher risk—whatever you created would never go away. Little would have happened.

People would ask me if this was the most creative company I had ever had. I'd say, "No, I've had this many creative people before; they just weren't allowed to write on the walls."

Many young companies are trying out unusual spaces. For instance, Spanish architecture firm Selgas Cano's office, located in a forest near Madrid, resembles a large subway car. Situated half above ground and half below, the office offers views into the forest through one Plexiglas side.

Then there's clothing maker Comvert, whose new headquarters is in a former movie theater. In order to take advantage of the excess vertical space that the cinema offered, the company built a suspended skate bowl above its warehouse. And in so-called Silicon Roundabout in London's East End, the social-media company Grape Digital works in the retrofitted Marie Lloyd Pub (named after the Victorian music-hall singer). This environment has not only boosted productivity, but the company found that few prospective clients would turn down a meeting in a pub.

The writing is on the wall

Through years of experience I've discovered that letting people write all over the walls, in any medium, promotes creativity. Most creative types think in terms of broad strokes. They are often limited by the space available on a piece of paper or a computer monitor. Moreover, drawing while talking to someone helps communicate complex ideas.

Now I install huge white boards and/or chalk boards everywhere in my companies. In one, we painted every wall with blackboard paint, some green and some black. The building shouted *creative!* to everyone, workers and visitors alike.

INTRODUCTION
MAKE YOUR WORKPLACE AN ADVERTISEMENT
FOR YOUR COMPANY ADOPT FLEXIBLE PONGS
ADVERTISE CREATIVELY HIRE FOR PASSION
AND INTENSITY IGNORE CREDENTIALS LOOK
FOR HOBBIES USE EMPLOYEES AS RESOURCES
AVOID THE CLONES HIRE THE OBNOXIOUS HIRE
THE CRAZY FIND THE BULLIED LOOK FOR THE
LURKERS ASK ABOUT BOOKS SAIL A BOAT HIRE
UNDER YOUR NOSE COMB THROUGH TWEETS
VISIT CREATIVE COMMUNITIES BEWARE OF
POSEURS ASK ODD QUESTIONS CONDUCT DEEP
INTERVIEWS CELEBRATE INSTITUTE A DEGREE OF
ANARCHY PROMOTE PRANKSTERISM SKUNK IT
UP FOSTER FAIRNESS ISOLATE CHAMPION THE
BAD IDEAS CELEBRATE FAILURE REQUIRE RISK
REWARD TURKEYS MENTOR TREAT EMPLOYEES
AS ADULTS CREATE A CREATIVE CHAIN CREATE
A CREATIVE SPACE **DESIGNATE A DEMO DAY**
ENCOURAGE ADHD PRELOAD LEARN TO
TALK CREATIVE THINK TOYS NEUTRALIZE THE
NAYSAYERS WRITE DOWN OBJECTIONS TAKE
CREATIVESTOCREATIVEPLACESMAKESOMETHING
FOR THE RICH CHANGE EVERY DAY, EVERY
HOUR THROW THE DICE DUCK PROCESSES
TAKE A RANDOM WALK THROUGH WIKIPEDIA
DON'T COUNT ON ACCOUNTING INVENT
HAPHAZARD HOLIDAYS MIX IT UP GO TO SLEEP
CONCLUSION

35

The problem: Creatives often go down their own personal rabbit holes and fail to finish their projects on time.

The solution: demo day.

Demo day is an artifice that both Steve Jobs and I used frequently. It started at Atari and has become a part of Silicon Valley culture.

In the tech world, and probably in many others, 90 percent of progress happens a week before a trade show (or in the case of other businesses, any deadline day). You can procrastinate and procrastinate, and then, finally, eventually, you act. But too often, you don't act fast enough—and you miss your deadline.

So at Atari we created soft deadlines called demo days. People were commanded to get their product into a completed-enough state such that everyone could see it, think about it, and critique it. Often, just to add some verisimilitude, we made up reasons for the imaginary deadlines, which were generally about two weeks away: a distributor from China was coming in, a venture capitalist wanted to see our work, a journalist was writing an article.

At Apple, Steve Jobs drove the concept to an even higher level. He would commission many designs for the same product, have them all demoed at the same time, choose which features he liked from the bunch, and then move the project forward to its actual completion date.

It doesn't matter what your project is—a marketing campaign, a website, or a movie—whatever you're starting to work on, in the beginning your knowledge of the actual task is incomplete. Only by working through the project can you flesh out the details.

In software development, for example, every project is written twice. When I was a programmer I would get 90 percent through the programs, finally get my "aha!" moment, abandon everything I had already done, and start again with my new vision. A novelist friend of mine finds that he has to throw out more than half of what he's written before he's done, because it takes him that long to really understand what it is he's writing.

In other words, create a soft deadline to help your creatives make the hard ones.

INTRODUCTION MAKE YOUR WORKPLACE AN ADVERTISEMENT FOR YOUR COMPANY ADOPT FLEXIBLE PONGS ADVERTISE CREATIVELY HIRE FOR PASSION AND INTENSITY IGNORE CREDENTIALS LOOK FOR HOBBIES USE EMPLOYEES AS RESOURCES AVOID THE CLONES HIRE THE OBNOXIOUS HIRE THE CRAZY FIND THE BULLIED LOOK FOR THE LURKERS ASK ABOUT BOOKS SAIL A BOAT HIRE UNDER YOUR NOSE COMB THROUGH TWEETS VISIT CREATIVE COMMUNITIES BEWARE OF POSEURS ASK ODD QUESTIONS CONDUCT DEEP INTERVIEWS CELEBRATE INSTITUTE A DEGREE OF ANARCHY PROMOTE PRANKSTERISM SKUNK IT UP FOSTER FAIRNESS ISOLATE CHAMPION THE BAD IDEAS CELEBRATE FAILURE REQUIRE RISK REWARD TURKEYS MENTOR TREAT EMPLOYEES AS ADULTS CREATE A CREATIVE CHAIN CREATE A CREATIVE SPACE DESIGNATE A DEMO DAY **ENCOURAGE ADHD** *PRELOAD LEARN TO TALK CREATIVE THINK TOYS NEUTRALIZE THE NAYSAYERS WRITE DOWN OBJECTIONS TAKE CREATIVESTOCREATIVEPLACESMAKESOMETHING FOR THE RICH CHANGE EVERY DAY, EVERY HOUR THROW THE DICE DUCK PROCESSES TAKE A RANDOM WALK THROUGH WIKIPEDIA DON'T COUNT ON ACCOUNTING INVENT HAPHAZARD HOLIDAYS MIX IT UP GO TO SLEEP CONCLUSION*

36

Creatives and attention deficit hyperactivity disorder (ADHD) go together. This isn't as bad as it sounds. ADHD can have its advantages. Creatives' brains tend to be so active that if it were literally possible to open them up and watch the ideas, you'd see hundreds of them jumping up and down, clamoring for attention, little birds all demanding a worm. However, if someone actually attempted to work on all these ideas, the result would be countless unfed projects.

The obvious tack most managers take to deal with this frenetic mental activity is to keep their creatives focused on one project, which to most people sounds like a reasonable plan.

It's not. Limiting your creatives to one and only one project can be so frustrating to them that it hinders rather than helps their overall productivity. I've found that if you constrain your creatives to work on just one project, the resulting boredom they suffer is often relieved by surfing the web, reading a magazine, goofing off, and doing anything else they can think of to keep their active minds occupied, and they end up slacking off on that one goal you assigned them.

Instead, assign your creatives several projects at the same time—something you wouldn't do with the average person. When you give creatives multiple tasks, they tend to feel less limited and can often complete several of them in the same time frame in which they might have finished just one.

These people have tremendous bandwidth. Take advantage of it. They want you to. Keep them productive by giving them what others would think of as an impossible workload. (Bear in mind, this tactic only works if the tasking is soft, i.e., without deadlines. If you create strict deadlines, then you're adding an element of panic, which narrows the bandwidth. See pong 35.)

There is an interesting study reported in the book *Art & Fear* by David Bayles and Ted Orland. At a ceramics class, half the class was told they were to make one pot and would be graded on it. The other half was told that they would be graded on the number of pots they could make. Those who were tasked with making many pots turned out the best ones. Because they could experiment, have fun, and do whatever they wished, their level of risk was lower, and their pots were more interesting. Those doing one pot felt burdened by having their entire grade rest on the one project, so they refused to take chances and ended up making overly conservative choices with their creations.

I N T R O D U C T I O N
MAKE YOUR WORKPLACE AN ADVERTISEMENT
FOR YOUR COMPANY ADOPT FLEXIBLE PONGS
ADVERTISE CREATIVELY HIRE FOR PASSION
AND INTENSITY IGNORE CREDENTIALS LOOK
FOR HOBBIES USE EMPLOYEES AS RESOURCES
AVOID THE CLONES HIRE THE OBNOXIOUS HIRE
THE CRAZY FIND THE BULLIED LOOK FOR THE
LURKERS ASK ABOUT BOOKS SAIL A BOAT HIRE
UNDER YOUR NOSE COMB THROUGH TWEETS
VISIT CREATIVE COMMUNITIES BEWARE OF
POSEURS ASK ODD QUESTIONS CONDUCT DEEP
INTERVIEWS CELEBRATE INSTITUTE A DEGREE OF
ANARCHY PROMOTE PRANKSTERISM SKUNK IT
UP FOSTER FAIRNESS ISOLATE CHAMPION THE
BAD IDEAS CELEBRATE FAILURE REQUIRE RISK
REWARD TURKEYS MENTOR TREAT EMPLOYEES
AS ADULTS CREATE A CREATIVE CHAIN CREATE
A CREATIVE SPACE DESIGNATE A DEMO DAY
ENCOURAGE ADHD **PRELOAD** *LEARN TO*
TALK CREATIVE THINK TOYS NEUTRALIZE THE
NAYSAYERS WRITE DOWN OBJECTIONS TAKE
CREATIVESTOCREATIVEPLACESMAKESOMETHING
FOR THE RICH CHANGE EVERY DAY, EVERY
HOUR THROW THE DICE DUCK PROCESSES
TAKE A RANDOM WALK THROUGH WIKIPEDIA
DON'T COUNT ON ACCOUNTING INVENT
HAPHAZARD HOLIDAYS MIX IT UP GO TO SLEEP
C O N C L U S I O N

37

Most people will tell you they only want to know as much as they need to know at any given time. Not creatives. When tasking a group of creative people, give them a heads up on their next projects. Their endlessly functioning, hyperactive minds will immediately start thinking about the future, even as they are still working on their current projects.

We spend our days pleasantly unaware of how much information our brain is actually absorbing because that is how it is programmed to work. However, if I were to tell someone that her next project was going to focus on, say, fire hydrants, for the next six months she will notice every fire hydrant that she passes and she'll start to understand nuances and differences among the hydrants that would not have been possible without that prompt. She may not even be doing this consciously, but then again, we often don't know what our subconscious mind is doing. So even though the fire hydrant project won't start for some time, when it does, she'll already be ahead.

Most creatives want to drink steadily from the knowledge fire hose. The more you can satisfy that thirst, the happier they will be, and their outcomes will reflect their happiness.

An example: In 1974, we told the Atari engineering staff that, starting in six months, all of our games had to be easily adapted to European standards. However, they didn't have to do anything about it in the meantime. What we noticed was that once

161

we were ready to start working on the project, all the engineers already knew the European standards backwards and forwards and had ideas that could make the conversion process simple and cheap. What we thought would be a long and difficult project took less than a month to complete.

Much research substantiates the preloading technique. According to a 2009 study at the University of British Columbia, the part of the brain that solves complex problems is actually very active and runs in the background when we daydream or do mundane tasks. The study, substantiated by MRIs of brain activity, found that the so-called "executive network," or lateral prefrontal cortex, and the dorsal anterior cingulated cortex become activated when we use our minds this way.

The great French mathematician Henri Poincaré once described how he came to solve a difficult problem this way: "One morning, walking on the bluff, the idea came to me, with brevity, suddenness and immediate certainty. . . Most striking at first is this appearance of sudden illumination, a manifest sign of long, unconscious prior work. The role of unconscious work in mathematical invention appears to me incontestable."

Keep your creatives' minds busy. Make sure there's always unconscious work going on in their brains.

I N T R O D U C T I O N
MAKE YOUR WORKPLACE AN ADVERTISEMENT
FOR YOUR COMPANY ADOPT FLEXIBLE PONGS
ADVERTISE CREATIVELY HIRE FOR PASSION
AND INTENSITY IGNORE CREDENTIALS LOOK
FOR HOBBIES USE EMPLOYEES AS RESOURCES
AVOID THE CLONES HIRE THE OBNOXIOUS HIRE
THE CRAZY FIND THE BULLIED LOOK FOR THE
LURKERS ASK ABOUT BOOKS SAIL A BOAT HIRE
UNDER YOUR NOSE COMB THROUGH TWEETS
VISIT CREATIVE COMMUNITIES BEWARE OF
POSEURS ASK ODD QUESTIONS CONDUCT DEEP
INTERVIEWS CELEBRATE INSTITUTE A DEGREE OF
ANARCHY PROMOTE PRANKSTERISM SKUNK IT
UP FOSTER FAIRNESS ISOLATE CHAMPION THE
BAD IDEAS CELEBRATE FAILURE REQUIRE RISK
REWARD TURKEYS MENTOR TREAT EMPLOYEES
AS ADULTS CREATE A CREATIVE CHAIN CREATE
A CREATIVE SPACE DESIGNATE A DEMO DAY
ENCOURAGE ADHD PRELOAD **LEARN TO**
TALK CREATIVE *THINK TOYS NEUTRALIZE THE*
NAYSAYERS WRITE DOWN OBJECTIONS TAKE
CREATIVES TO CREATIVE PLACES MAKE SOMETHING
FOR THE RICH CHANGE EVERY DAY, EVERY
HOUR THROW THE DICE DUCK PROCESSES
TAKE A RANDOM WALK THROUGH WIKIPEDIA
DON'T COUNT ON ACCOUNTING INVENT
HAPHAZARD HOLIDAYS MIX IT UP GO TO SLEEP
C O N C L U S I O N

38

As mentioned, one of the characteristics of the true creative is a certain amount of intellectual arrogance. Steve Jobs thought everyone he reported to was, basically, an idiot. (Of course, I was one of those people.)

The point isn't who's smarter. It's not a contest. The point is to help these people create like crazy for you. One of the best ways to achieve this: Don't act like an idiot. Learn as much as you can about them. Learn what they do. And most of all, learn to speak their language.

In other words, if someone is working at some high level of technical knowledge, you need to be able, at a minimum, to have a conversation with him. For instance, if he's developing new software, knowing the difference between Python and Unix is necessary. This doesn't mean that you have to know a great deal about the subject, but it does mean you should be able to ask a great question—and understand much of the answer.

When the manager becomes the student, she gains respect. It gives your creatives the ability to strut a bit, to talk about what they know, and to show how smart they are—especially to their superiors, who in their minds may be all powerful but not all that bright.

A sincere show of interest is a salve to a confused soul. You will never be as good at whatever it is these people are doing. But to show some curiosity and some knowledge elevates you in their eyes from a moron to a fellow traveler in the knowledge space. There is often very little that's endearing about someone who wants to manage, but much to like about someone who wants to listen and learn.

INTRODUCTION MAKE YOUR WORKPLACE AN ADVERTISEMENT FOR YOUR COMPANY ADOPT FLEXIBLE PONGS ADVERTISE CREATIVELY HIRE FOR PASSION AND INTENSITY IGNORE CREDENTIALS LOOK FOR HOBBIES USE EMPLOYEES AS RESOURCES AVOID THE CLONES HIRE THE OBNOXIOUS HIRE THE CRAZY FIND THE BULLIED LOOK FOR THE LURKERS ASK ABOUT BOOKS SAIL A BOAT HIRE UNDER YOUR NOSE COMB THROUGH TWEETS VISIT CREATIVE COMMUNITIES BEWARE OF POSEURS ASK ODD QUESTIONS CONDUCT DEEP INTERVIEWS CELEBRATE INSTITUTE A DEGREE OF ANARCHY PROMOTE PRANKSTERISM SKUNK IT UP FOSTER FAIRNESS ISOLATE CHAMPION THE BAD IDEAS CELEBRATE FAILURE REQUIRE RISK REWARD TURKEYS MENTOR TREAT EMPLOYEES AS ADULTS CREATE A CREATIVE CHAIN CREATE A CREATIVE SPACE DESIGNATE A DEMO DAY ENCOURAGE ADHD PRELOAD LEARN TO TALK CREATIVE **THINK TOYS** NEUTRALIZE THE NAYSAYERS WRITE DOWN OBJECTIONS TAKE CREATIVES TO CREATIVE PLACES MAKE SOMETHING FOR THE RICH CHANGE EVERY DAY, EVERY HOUR THROW THE DICE DUCK PROCESSES TAKE A RANDOM WALK THROUGH WIKIPEDIA DON'T COUNT ON ACCOUNTING INVENT HAPHAZARD HOLIDAYS MIX IT UP GO TO SLEEP CONCLUSION

39

Creativity is unlocked only when people feel free to express it in as many ways as possible. At Atari, and many other companies, toys are always present at meetings and other gatherings. For example, the design firm IDEO (which designed the original mouse for Apple in 1980) encourages its employees to play with toys to spur imagination and stocks its offices with playthings, designed in house, called finger blasters, or NERF-like projectiles with a rubber band trigger that can fly up to 100 feet.

Playing with games, toys, and puzzles isn't just for fun in the moment. It can help both employees and managers in various ways. Games such as Go and chess force you to train your mind to think ahead, work through possible future moves, and think in more than two dimensions. Similarly, building toys such as LEGO allow you to practice starting with a small idea and slowly build it out into something large and unique.

Even toys such as squirt guns or darts can be useful (in moderation) to let people revert to childhood states, which is important. Too many of us have had our creativity trained out of us—it's too unruly, it doesn't conform. Edit yourselves, adults tell us when we are young, and so we do, so much so that most of us don't even realize we are doing it.

Toys give people permission to quit self-editing and think with the parts of our brains that have been squashed over the years. They let you play out ideas that bubble up from places that you've been told to ignore, like the deepest parts of your imagination.

For example, the first game I created was called *Computer Space*, and to realize it I needed a spacey-looking cabinet. So I sat down with my favorite toy at the time, modeling clay, added a piece of wood, cut out some Plexiglas for the screen, and modeled what I thought was a cool shape. It was good enough for me to show it to my partner, Ted Dabney, who found someone who was able to scale it up into fiberglass. Three weeks later, it became the first video game. I licensed it to a company called Nutting Associates and did about three million dollars in sales. The royalties allowed me to start Atari.

At my consumer electronics company Axlon, a group of us was once sitting in a conference room talking about a specific toy, trying to define some of its characteristics. Even as we talked about it, I noticed that at the far end of the table one of the engineers was actually building the thing—out of LEGO blocks. Just the shape, and not to scale, but he had gotten the essential idea from our discussion and was able to give us a vision of it. Someone else suggested the top should be wider, and soon everyone was creating the product collaboratively, with blocks.

Another time, at Chuck E. Cheese's, I was telling someone about a project for which we needed an arcade space that looked like a forest. It turned out this man had a collection of G.I. Joe action figures, which he then cobbled together with a hot-glue gun, masking tape, and cardboard, and presto! We had an amazingly accurate mock-up diorama. We knew the project was going to work before we ever built it.

Let your employees self-curate their own toy collection—you lose the element of surprise and fun if the company takes complete control of the process. But the company can start it. Begin with a basket of LEGO blocks on the conference table. Next, add some Plasticine or Play-Doh—in other words, include toys that are clean and easy to manipulate and throw back into the box. Allow people to take the toys back to their offices to play with after the meeting. Don't worry about losing pieces; the company should feel good about replenishing the basket. Let the toys proliferate through the building.

Not surprisingly, the Danish-based LEGO Group allows its employees the right to play with its signature blocks whenever they'd like—the company even installed podiums so employees can display their creations.

INTRODUCTION MAKE YOUR WORKPLACE AN ADVERTISEMENT FOR YOUR COMPANY ADOPT FLEXIBLE PONGS ADVERTISE CREATIVELY HIRE FOR PASSION AND INTENSITY IGNORE CREDENTIALS LOOK FOR HOBBIES USE EMPLOYEES AS RESOURCES AVOID THE CLONES HIRE THE OBNOXIOUS HIRE THE CRAZY FIND THE BULLIED LOOK FOR THE LURKERS ASK ABOUT BOOKS SAIL A BOAT HIRE UNDER YOUR NOSE COMB THROUGH TWEETS VISIT CREATIVE COMMUNITIES BEWARE OF POSEURS ASK ODD QUESTIONS CONDUCT DEEP INTERVIEWS CELEBRATE INSTITUTE A DEGREE OF ANARCHY PROMOTE PRANKSTERISM SKUNK IT UP FOSTER FAIRNESS ISOLATE CHAMPION THE BAD IDEAS CELEBRATE FAILURE REQUIRE RISK REWARD TURKEYS MENTOR TREAT EMPLOYEES AS ADULTS CREATE A CREATIVE CHAIN CREATE A CREATIVE SPACE DESIGNATE A DEMO DAY ENCOURAGE ADHD PRELOAD LEARN TO TALK CREATIVE THINK TOYS **NEUTRALIZE THE NAYSAYERS** WRITE DOWN OBJECTIONS TAKE CREATIVES TO CREATIVE PLACES MAKE SOMETHING FOR THE RICH CHANGE EVERY DAY, EVERY HOUR THROW THE DICE DUCK PROCESSES TAKE A RANDOM WALK THROUGH WIKIPEDIA DON'T COUNT ON ACCOUNTING INVENT HAPHAZARD HOLIDAYS MIX IT UP GO TO SLEEP CONCLUSION

40

There are many obstacles to creativity, but one of the most pernicious is other people. There's an old saying, "The good ideas end up on the cutting-room floor." How do they generally end up there? Because other people have taken those good ideas and thrown them away.

(There's also another saying, attributed to philosopher Jean-Paul Sartre: "Hell is other people." That one needs no explanation.)

Who are these other people? They are those naysayers who somehow manage to permeate every company like termites infest old buildings. I have seldom seen a company that did not have its fair share of these people, including my own. The trick is not to let them in. But if they're already infesting your company, you need to find them and neutralize them.

These naysayers are easy to spot because they're the ones who prevent projects from taking off, who quash creativity, who sap imagination. They've gained power and prestige by being the company curmudgeon. They pretend that they're doing this or that for the company's good (someone has to play devil's advocate, they say). But they're really saying no all the time because it's all they know how to do, and because they have no ideas of their own.

In fact, they continue to thrive because they never stick their neck out and thus exist in the glow of their perfect record.

When you give your approval to a new idea, like it or not, you have just taken on some responsibility for a possible failure. But if all you ever do is shoot down project after project, you are always going to be 100 percent correct. Nothing upon which you have your stamp fails because you haven't stamped anything. This does not make you smart. This makes you obstructive.

There was only one word we outlawed at Atari: no. I wouldn't let people say it. Any idiot can say no. There's no mental process there. If you don't like something, the trick is to think of something better.

If people didn't feel comfortable with a new idea, I would allow them to think only about how the project could be better, or come up with ways to turn their apprehension into enthusiasm. Not only did this policy save people from just stamping a "no" on projects, it forced an atmosphere of collective problem solving. Suddenly, even the naysayers had to find ways to be imaginative, creative, and articulate enough to turn a no into a yes.

I found it quite funny to watch this group scamper to try to become problem solvers when they realized that the gig was up. And I also found that when one of their ilk was fired, the others attempted to become helpful. Of course, they had been vacuous for such a long time that they were not particularly good at anything beyond saying no.

Note: As mentioned in pong 32, creative people are seldom good communicators. In fact, it's a general rule that your communicative people aren't necessarily creative, and your creative people aren't communicative. Glibness isn't intelligence. Often managers say no to an idea because the person trying to explain it simply isn't very good at the process. Never let great ideas disappear because managers say no before the idea is fully explained.

INTRODUCTION MAKE YOUR WORKPLACE AN ADVERTISEMENT FOR YOUR COMPANY ADOPT FLEXIBLE PONGS ADVERTISE CREATIVELY HIRE FOR PASSION AND INTENSITY IGNORE CREDENTIALS LOOK FOR HOBBIES USE EMPLOYEES AS RESOURCES AVOID THE CLONES HIRE THE OBNOXIOUS HIRE THE CRAZY FIND THE BULLIED LOOK FOR THE LURKERS ASK ABOUT BOOKS SAIL A BOAT HIRE UNDER YOUR NOSE COMB THROUGH TWEETS VISIT CREATIVE COMMUNITIES BEWARE OF POSEURS ASK ODD QUESTIONS CONDUCT DEEP INTERVIEWS CELEBRATE INSTITUTE A DEGREE OF ANARCHY PROMOTE PRANKSTERISM SKUNK IT UP FOSTER FAIRNESS ISOLATE CHAMPION THE BAD IDEAS CELEBRATE FAILURE REQUIRE RISK REWARD TURKEYS MENTOR TREAT EMPLOYEES AS ADULTS CREATE A CREATIVE CHAIN CREATE A CREATIVE SPACE DESIGNATE A DEMO DAY ENCOURAGE ADHD PRELOAD LEARN TO TALK CREATIVE THINK TOYS NEUTRALIZE THE NAYSAYERS **WRITE DOWN OBJECTIONS** TAKE CREATIVES TO CREATIVE PLACES MAKE SOMETHING FOR THE RICH CHANGE EVERY DAY, EVERY HOUR THROW THE DICE DUCK PROCESSES TAKE A RANDOM WALK THROUGH WIKIPEDIA DON'T COUNT ON ACCOUNTING INVENT HAPHAZARD HOLIDAYS MIX IT UP GO TO SLEEP CONCLUSION

41

Every single day, throughout the world of business, truly creative ideas are being mercilessly killed. Each one deserves a moment of mourning. Without good ideas, the future won't unfold the way we want it to—a strong tomorrow can't be built on a foundation of weak concepts. So the goal is to stop all these good ideas from being murdered.

One of the best ways to do that is relatively simple: Ask people to write down their objections to ideas. Why? Because it's too easy to kill an idea verbally. Thinking they have to speak up when presented with a new idea, people do, and they almost always feel more comfortable criticizing it than praising it. That's just human nature. It's always easier to say no than yes.

A much better tactic is to ask that objections be written down. When people write critiques, with their name attached, they are forced to take personal responsibility for their negative opinions. They are on record saying that they don't think the project will work. If it then goes forward, and is successful, their prognostication skills are in doubt—whereas if they simply voiced their opinion, they could always claim they were misheard, or that they were just echoing someone else, or offer some other excuse.

To increase creativity, you must decrease the number of ways your company says no. Yet at most companies, the people with the most power regarding the success or failure of a project tend to be the ones who can analyze it least intelligently. But if they are held responsible for their criticism, they're less likely to so easily offer it.

The other advantage to writing down objections is that you can circulate them, allowing the rest of the employees to contribute their ideas as well. And, you force people to be more specific. If the worst part of an idea is its cost, writing down actual numbers forces people to be more precise in their estimates, and gives the idea's creator a chance to be more precise in her rebuttal as well.

Finally, when people give quick voice to their objections, those objections aren't generally thoughtful. The pressure is to speak, not to be accurate. A written statement forces people to explain exactly what they mean, with the proper analytics.

For example: Several years ago I was brought into a company as a creative consultant. I even held a creative session at Pajaro Dunes (see pong 26), thinking it would be as productive as my earlier sessions there.

It wasn't. The hostility to creativity at this company was almost dripping from the walls. But it didn't come from everyone. It took only an hour to identify the problem managers (three of the eleven employees). If it had been my company, I would have fired the lot right there.

That was not my place. Instead, I decided to trap them. I handed out paper and pens and asked everyone to list the company's products about which they were most and least enthusiastic. Once they were done, I told them to list how they could make the projects better or, if they were against them, how they could tweak them to make them work.

What I wanted them to do was be creative in the most positive way—and without any wiggle room.

Many managers hate that. But good managers who want to hire and nurture creatives are more than happy to engage in the process of inventing something new and wonderful. Helping to refine an idea is as important as having the idea itself.

After making my assignment, I then gave everyone thirty

minutes to write down their issues and ideas. No collaboration was allowed. I also told everyone that I was about to take a walk on the beach, and if anyone needed to talk to me, they could.

The three toxic managers all stepped out and asked me for further instructions and guidance and, frankly, attempted to shine me on.

As I expected, there were some excellent ideas offered by the eight good managers, and nothing but trash from the three toxics. The saddest part was that the toxics all occupied elevated management positions. It's often true—and sad—that these people, not being good at creativity, are excellent at office politics. They thrive not because of their ideas but because they know how to thrive. Toxics are more concerned about what's right for them and their careers than they are about the well-being of the company.

When we reconvened, I told the group that although many of the suggestions were quite good, there were also a smaller number of poor ones. I limited my discussion to the five best.

I then told the group that the next time we did this exercise I would read the best ideas and identify the authors aloud to everyone. Getting rid of anonymity ups the risk for non-creatives. Their worst fear is that they may be fingered as the empty-suit managers that they are.

It worked like a charm. All the toxics became amazingly helpful and paid closer attention to the group than they had before—they knew that they could not simply pontificate but actually had to compete in idea creation with their subordinates. They had no place to hide.

In my later conversations with the company's CEO, I related the process I'd used at these sessions. He laughed and said that everyone had raved about the retreat except the three toxics.

Naysayers vs. toxics

They may sound similar, but these types of employees are two different categories of trouble. The bad news: Some people are both.

Naysayers (see pong 40) reject before analyzing. They don't want to say yes. They love to say no. Naysayers are recipe players—they know the formula for what has worked in the past, and they have thrived in that framework. They do not want to change it. Change is dangerous. The best way to stop change from happening is to say no as many times as possible.

Example: After Atari was sold to Warner Communications, I found myself surrounded by executive naysayers who proceeded to dismantle Atari's creative culture, terminating all the research projects that were not totally aligned with the previous year's product line. It was recipe playing at its worst—these people wanted what had worked already, not what was going to work in the future.

Toxics are more dangerous—and often harder to recognize. They constantly reframe every possible new development at the company into one that is good for them—without any interest in whether or not it's good for the company. If the company tanks, they can always get a new job, since they're constantly working on their résumés and their contacts. They don't care. They don't work for the company. They work for themselves. Toxics are supremely subtle, preternaturally political, and potentially psychopathic. Rehabilitate or exterminate them.

I N T R O D U C T I O N
MAKE YOUR WORKPLACE AN ADVERTISEMENT
FOR YOUR COMPANY ADOPT FLEXIBLE PONGS
ADVERTISE CREATIVELY HIRE FOR PASSION
AND INTENSITY IGNORE CREDENTIALS LOOK
FOR HOBBIES USE EMPLOYEES AS RESOURCES
AVOID THE CLONES HIRE THE OBNOXIOUS HIRE
THE CRAZY FIND THE BULLIED LOOK FOR THE
LURKERS ASK ABOUT BOOKS SAIL A BOAT HIRE
UNDER YOUR NOSE COMB THROUGH TWEETS
VISIT CREATIVE COMMUNITIES BEWARE OF
POSEURS ASK ODD QUESTIONS CONDUCT DEEP
INTERVIEWS CELEBRATE INSTITUTE A DEGREE OF
ANARCHY PROMOTE PRANKSTERISM SKUNK IT
UP FOSTER FAIRNESS ISOLATE CHAMPION THE
BAD IDEAS CELEBRATE FAILURE REQUIRE RISK
REWARD TURKEYS MENTOR TREAT EMPLOYEES
AS ADULTS CREATE A CREATIVE CHAIN CREATE
A CREATIVE SPACE DESIGNATE A DEMO DAY
ENCOURAGE ADHD PRELOAD LEARN TO
TALK CREATIVE THINK TOYS NEUTRALIZE THE
*NAYSAYERS WRITE DOWN OBJECTIONS **TAKE***
***CREATIVES TO CREATIVE PLACES** MAKE SOMETHING*
FOR THE RICH CHANGE EVERY DAY, EVERY
HOUR THROW THE DICE DUCK PROCESSES
TAKE A RANDOM WALK THROUGH WIKIPEDIA
DON'T COUNT ON ACCOUNTING INVENT
HAPHAZARD HOLIDAYS MIX IT UP GO TO SLEEP
C O N C L U S I O N

42

Back when Atari was booming, most American cities had two to three major distributors in the coin-operated game business, separated by product lines. Game companies tended to have an exclusive in each city. That meant the guy across the street from Atari's distributor in, say, Chicago, would always be trying to get someone to go into business against us.

When we realized that no one else was stepping up to do this, we thought, why not become our own competitor? So we created a company called Key Games, which was actually 100 percent owned by Atari but was set up to look as though it were our competitor. The salespeople from Key Games next went to the second-strongest distributor in each city and became its game supplier. We then took every other game from our engineering department, moved it over to Key Games, and soon Key Games was doing very well. Between Atari and Key Games, we ended up with an 80 percent market share.

This hugely successful idea came out of a meeting held in a hot tub. I had recently hired a new marketing director and, given that it was a beautiful day, we decided to sit outside in the hot tub at my house in Los Gatos, California, to discuss marketing problems.

Many other excellent ideas arose out of soaking ourselves in this relaxed and calm place.

You can't do that in today's workplace. Hot tubs are a relic of the 1970s. So think up alternatives to a hot tub and immerse your company in them. It can be anything. For example, brain research shows that if you can talk and walk at the same time, you're more likely to come up with ideas. Or, think and groom: Albert Einstein once said that many of his greatest ideas came to him while he was shaving, and that he had to be very careful when he put the blade to his flesh or he might cut himself when surprised by a great idea.

In 1969, Gestalt psychologist Wolfgang Köhler gave a famous lecture in which he discussed the three Bs of creativity—"the bus, the bath, and the bed"—the environments where creative insights often appear. (Köhler was specifically referring to three renowned instances of spontaneous creativity, the bath being where Greek philosopher Archimedes discovered the law of physics relating to buoyancy force; the bed where German chemist Friedrich August Kekulé dreamed up his insight about electronic bonding in benzene molecules; the bus, where mathematician Henri Poincaré came up with one of his most important mathematical discoveries.)

I've also had great ideas strike in or on one of the three Bs, as have many of my employees. In fact, I've found that just by moving people around, getting them to work in different environments, we enabled them to come up with many creative new ideas. So I often used to take employees skiing, to the beach, to the mountains, anywhere I thought their minds might benefit from the experience.

One of the most important ideas for Chuck E. Cheese's was developed when we realized that we hadn't created enough to do for kids who weren't old enough to play the games—and if they weren't happy, their parents would leave and never return. So we developed the concept of a playground with ball crawls. That idea came out of a fireside chat following a day of skiing.

The business plan for the Etak navigation system (the first company to digitize world maps) was written over the chart table in my sailboat in the middle of the Pacific Ocean. I was sailing with my friend, engineer Stan Honey, and we were waiting for a satellite navigational fix, which back then you could only receive when a satellite was directly overhead. (Stan is an amazing inventor; one of his best is those artificial lines on football fields that you see on your television screen—these are so realistic that many people think those lines actually exist on the fields themselves.)

Between midnight and 4 a.m., Stan and I were working on some navigational issues, talking about the difference between navigating on land and on sea and ways to make both easier. In that cramped little cabin, under low lights, fueled by gallons of coffee, we riffed on new kinds of automobile navigation until we solved the challenge. What we came up with—Etak's Navigator—was the first commercially available automotive navigation system of any practical significance. We also created digital maps and mapping software, selling the company to Rupert Murdoch's News Corp. in 1989.

Many other companies have learned the benefits of moving their creatives out of the office to places where inspiration is more likely to strike. For example, Hallmark's Specialty Creative Division was flourishing until the 1980s, when the company's profitability, and creativity, plummeted. In 1994, a new creative director was hired with the directive to put a new creative chain in place. He gave his employees 30 percent of the division's time and resources to recharge—they could take sabbaticals, research trips to Europe, pursue hobbies on company time, or just wander off to a newly created retreat on a nearby farm.

It worked. Net revenues rose steadily after the changes, from $3 billion in 1994 to $3.7 billion in 1997. Today, the privately held company is an approximately $4.1 billion business.

Don't force your creatives to spend all day at a desk. The more interesting and creative environments you place them in, the more likely they are to come up with interesting and creative ideas.

43

Many times people begin the creative process with the best intentions but, nonetheless, feel burdened with an immediate and limiting proviso. They want to make a terrific product or service, they say, but. . . it has to be one that everyone can afford.

This seems logical—how can you reach a wide market if the price of your product is prohibitive? So when companies do their numbers and see the potential costs, they assume that without a large commercial market, they can't take the project forward. And thus terrific ideas are thrown away for fear of an admission price that seems too high.

The truth is that it's quite appropriate to make a terrific product/service for the wealthy. In their early years, many successful products have been very expensive.

So try a different approach. Say: I will build this only for rich people, who have money to burn. If you think that way, you free up one of the major self-constraints people place on creativity.

The fact is, the project may or may not end up costing consumers as much as you might first assume. Often ideas that initially seem cost-prohibitive end up being cost-advantageous because the more the team learns about a project the more cost savings it can inject into it.

But even if the project does end up being pricey, keep in mind that the road to innovation often travels through the wealthiest neighborhoods. The rich were the only people able to afford the first telephones, the first airplanes, the first cars, the first computers, and so on. The wealthy are always looking for new products to make their lives easier, more enjoyable, or more productive, and creative minds are there to invent them.

If the product is good, its price generally plummets. Items prohibitively expensive in the past are sold at discounts today. Take the bicycle: In the 1860s, a Parisian blacksmith named Pierre Michaux began selling custom bicycles with pedals for what was then a pricey 250 francs. Most of his first customers were nobles, and the bicycle remained a high-priced toy for moneyed young men until the early part of the twentieth century, when department stores like Sears finally found ways to make and sell them inexpensively. (If you tore your clothes riding, you were lucky if you had a sewing machine to fix them; such machines were a lavish expense for most people in the nineteenth century, selling for $125 when the average annual income was $500. But by the mid-twentieth century, 85 percent of all American households owned one.)

Similarly, the microwave oven, invented by Percy L. Spencer and first sold in 1947, was about six feet tall and weighed 750 pounds, looking more like a refrigerator than today's compact unit. It cost the modern equivalent of about thirty thousand dollars and was sold only to commercial customers. Even the first consumer models, sold in the mid-1950s, were priced up to today's equivalent of fifteen thousand dollars. Today, more than 90 percent of American households own a microwave oven.

To give a more recent example, IBM's Watson computer is a three-million-dollar supercomputer that is capable of understanding human language and, in 2011, even won an episode of the quiz show *Jeopardy*. The computer is currently being used on a trial basis in the health care industry to help medical professionals research and treat cancer. However, there is talk that within a few years the company might be able to create a pocket-sized, consumer version of the product—at a fraction of its current multimillion-dollar cost.

Create something that allows the middle class to act like the rich, and you may have a hit. That's one of the reasons the driverless car will be so successful: Middle-class drivers will have the equivalent of a chauffeur, getting dropped off at the curb while the car then leaves and parks itself. Everyone except chauffeurs will be happy.

within a few years the company might be able to create a pocket...

INTRODUCTION
MAKE YOUR WORKPLACE AN ADVERTISEMENT
FOR YOUR COMPANY ADOPT FLEXIBLE PONGS
ADVERTISE CREATIVELY HIRE FOR PASSION
AND INTENSITY IGNORE CREDENTIALS LOOK
FOR HOBBIES USE EMPLOYEES AS RESOURCES
AVOID THE CLONES HIRE THE OBNOXIOUS HIRE
THE CRAZY FIND THE BULLIED LOOK FOR THE
LURKERS ASK ABOUT BOOKS SAIL A BOAT HIRE
UNDER YOUR NOSE COMB THROUGH TWEETS
VISIT CREATIVE COMMUNITIES BEWARE OF
POSEURS ASK ODD QUESTIONS CONDUCT DEEP
INTERVIEWS CELEBRATE INSTITUTE A DEGREE OF
ANARCHY PROMOTE PRANKSTERISM SKUNK IT
UP FOSTER FAIRNESS ISOLATE CHAMPION THE
BAD IDEAS CELEBRATE FAILURE REQUIRE RISK
REWARD TURKEYS MENTOR TREAT EMPLOYEES
AS ADULTS CREATE A CREATIVE CHAIN CREATE
A CREATIVE SPACE DESIGNATE A DEMO DAY
ENCOURAGE ADHD PRELOAD LEARN TO
TALK CREATIVE THINK TOYS NEUTRALIZE THE
NAYSAYERS WRITE DOWN OBJECTIONS TAKE
CREATIVES TO CREATIVE PLACES MAKE SOMETHING
FOR THE RICH ***CHANGE EVERY DAY, EVERY***
HOUR *THROW THE DICE DUCK PROCESSES*
TAKE A RANDOM WALK THROUGH WIKIPEDIA
DON'T COUNT ON ACCOUNTING INVENT
HAPHAZARD HOLIDAYS MIX IT UP GO TO SLEEP
CONCLUSION

44

In the 1980s, musician Frank Zappa felt that he was going through a creative dry spell, so he came up with a plan. Instead of getting up at the same time every morning, each day he rose one hour later than the day before. This means that twelve days later, he was getting up at 8 p.m., having breakfast, working, eating lunch around 1 a.m., going to sleep around noon, and getting up the next day at 9 p.m., and so on. This behavior pattern, he said, helped him come up with fresh ideas. How could he not see things in a new way? His whole life was now new.

Get your creatives to emulate Frank—not necessarily in terms of their daily schedule, as this might make the office a little difficult to manage—but in terms of shaking up their lives. Find as many ways as possible to keep their minds active and flexible. Encourage them to find a new route to work every day, or get them to walk, or bicycle, or skateboard instead. Have them drive through different neighborhoods, shop at new stores, walk through places they've never been before, stop and say hello to different people. Ask them to experiment with new foods, add new words to their vocabulary, try new glasses frames, wear different clothes. Instead of casual Fridays, have wear-something-you've-never-worn-before Fridays. Give employees odd working hours. Let them go crazy with their office spaces. Tell them to turn their chairs around and sit on them backward, rearrange their desktops, lie on the floor. The idea is to get people's brains working in as many different ways as possible, to shake off the shackles of the norm.

The habits of highly effective people are seldom creative; highly habitual people don't tend to have original ideas. They're trying to have a well-planned life. When all you want is execution, consistency can be an excellent thing. But when you want wild, off-the-wall, uninhibited creativity, it is a spoiler.

As for myself, when I am in execution mode, I become highly focused and fall back on tried-and-true routine. But in my creative mode, I become as unregimented as possible: I change my hours, become more of a night person, and the ideas start to flow.

What you are really trying to do with all the change-ups is jog the brain to thinking down different pathways. The brain doesn't want to do that. Design an environment for your creatives that makes their brains work harder, think differently, invent interestingly. The greater the uniformity, the greater the sameness. The greater the change, the greater the difference.

INTRODUCTION
MAKE YOUR WORKPLACE AN ADVERTISEMENT
FOR YOUR COMPANY ADOPT FLEXIBLE PONGS
ADVERTISE CREATIVELY HIRE FOR PASSION
AND INTENSITY IGNORE CREDENTIALS LOOK
FOR HOBBIES USE EMPLOYEES AS RESOURCES
AVOID THE CLONES HIRE THE OBNOXIOUS HIRE
THE CRAZY FIND THE BULLIED LOOK FOR THE
LURKERS ASK ABOUT BOOKS SAIL A BOAT HIRE
UNDER YOUR NOSE COMB THROUGH TWEETS
VISIT CREATIVE COMMUNITIES BEWARE OF
POSEURS ASK ODD QUESTIONS CONDUCT DEEP
INTERVIEWS CELEBRATE INSTITUTE A DEGREE OF
ANARCHY PROMOTE PRANKSTERISM SKUNK IT
UP FOSTER FAIRNESS ISOLATE CHAMPION THE
BAD IDEAS CELEBRATE FAILURE REQUIRE RISK
REWARD TURKEYS MENTOR TREAT EMPLOYEES
AS ADULTS CREATE A CREATIVE CHAIN CREATE
A CREATIVE SPACE DESIGNATE A DEMO DAY
ENCOURAGE ADHD PRELOAD LEARN TO
TALK CREATIVE THINK TOYS NEUTRALIZE THE
NAYSAYERS WRITE DOWN OBJECTIONS TAKE
CREATIVES TO CREATIVE PLACES MAKE SOMETHING
FOR THE RICH CHANGE EVERY DAY, EVERY
HOUR **THROW THE DICE** *DUCK PROCESSES*
TAKE A RANDOM WALK THROUGH WIKIPEDIA
DON'T COUNT ON ACCOUNTING INVENT
HAPHAZARD HOLIDAYS MIX IT UP GO TO SLEEP
CONCLUSION

45

In 1971, author George Cockcroft, writing under the pen name Luke Rhinehart, published a so-called autobiographical novel called *The Dice Man*, in which he explained how he used dice to make every important decision in his life. Although the novel was very successful—the BBC called it one of the fifty most influential books of the last half of the twentieth century—the idea of using dice to make important decisions has never really caught on. (Unless you count a recent Discovery Channel show called *The Diceman*, in which the hosts use dice to decide where they'll go and what they'll do.)

I think it should catch on. Rolling the dice to decide what you want to do is a terrific idea. Why? Because we all tend to self-select our agenda without being aware that we're doing so. For example, if you're the sort who makes list of things you need to work on, it is likely that you will unconsciously follow the same patterns you always do in response to that to-do list. Perhaps you will prioritize the ones that are very easy, or that interest you the most, or that you can get others to help you with. Whatever you choose, it reflects a pattern that has dictated your life.

What you don't realize is that because we all tend to make the same choices over and over, we all fall into our own private ruts. These ruts do not lead to creativity. Ruts lead to doing the same things, in the same ways, over and over—it's a vicious cycle.

So I encourage companies to try using dice now and then. If

you use dice as a randomizer, you've taken away your volition and you will obtain a different outcome than you otherwise would get by organizing according to your natural desires.

You'll also find that there are certain tasks you have put off without being fully aware that you're doing so. If you give the dice power, you won't be able to procrastinate any longer.

Here's how I do it: I create a list of possible agendas, and then number the items to correspond with the sides of the dice. Roll, and if the dice tell me to do number 12, I have to do number 12. I use my set of *Dungeons and Dragons* dice because they're twenty-sided. That means I can include on the list any number of things I don't really want to do, or never considered important before. And yet many times after I've listed these offbeat items, when the dice have selected them, I've found that getting them done has had a surprising and significant effect on my life.

This book's existence is an example of rolling the dice. Not long ago I decided that I needed to do something to build my brain, to get myself moving in a new direction. So I grabbed my dice and wrote down the options: go sky diving, climb Mt. Kilimanjaro, live in India for a month, study my favorite game (Go) with a master in Japan, write a book, and so on. There was no question in my mind that whatever the dice told me to do, I would do. But I rolled the "write the book" option, and so I set out to make that happen.

I love what a roll of the dice can accomplish. There are so many different paths our lives can take—and yet we are only peripherally aware of them. We need to explore those outlying places, and if you don't quite have the nerve to do so, then roll the dice and let them open up new vistas of capability and interest. Playing the dice game will exponentially increase the richness of your existence.

INTRODUCTION
MAKE YOUR WORKPLACE AN ADVERTISEMENT
FOR YOUR COMPANY ADOPT FLEXIBLE PONGS
ADVERTISE CREATIVELY HIRE FOR PASSION
AND INTENSITY IGNORE CREDENTIALS LOOK
FOR HOBBIES USE EMPLOYEES AS RESOURCES
AVOID THE CLONES HIRE THE OBNOXIOUS HIRE
THE CRAZY FIND THE BULLIED LOOK FOR THE
LURKERS ASK ABOUT BOOKS SAIL A BOAT HIRE
UNDER YOUR NOSE COMB THROUGH TWEETS
VISIT CREATIVE COMMUNITIES BEWARE OF
POSEURS ASK ODD QUESTIONS CONDUCT DEEP
INTERVIEWS CELEBRATE INSTITUTE A DEGREE OF
ANARCHY PROMOTE PRANKSTERISM SKUNK IT
UP FOSTER FAIRNESS ISOLATE CHAMPION THE
BAD IDEAS CELEBRATE FAILURE REQUIRE RISK
REWARD TURKEYS MENTOR TREAT EMPLOYEES
AS ADULTS CREATE A CREATIVE CHAIN CREATE
A CREATIVE SPACE DESIGNATE A DEMO DAY
ENCOURAGE ADHD PRELOAD LEARN TO
TALK CREATIVE THINK TOYS NEUTRALIZE THE
NAYSAYERS WRITE DOWN OBJECTIONS TAKE
CREATIVES TO CREATIVE PLACES MAKE SOMETHING
FOR THE RICH CHANGE EVERY DAY, EVERY
HOUR THROW THE DICE **DUCK PROCESSES**
TAKE A RANDOM WALK THROUGH WIKIPEDIA
DON'T COUNT ON ACCOUNTING INVENT
HAPHAZARD HOLIDAYS MIX IT UP GO TO SLEEP
CONCLUSION

46

Over the long run—if you're lucky enough to have a long run—every company develops a balancing act between process and outcome. This reality conforms to the rule of unintended consequences, which says that well-meaning, purposeful actions can often result in completely unexpected results. The concept has existed since humans started planning, but was popularized in the last century by the sociologist Robert K. Merton. In the case of modern business, the rule might go: The more you create organizational structure, the more likely it is your processes will become counterproductive. Otherwise, all the processes in the world would be useful and good. They're not.

For example, if your company adopts a rule that says all purchases have to be processed through the purchasing department, you might be adding something between five days to a month to your purchasing cycle. If someone at the company needs a part quickly, she will have to fill out a form and wait for it to go through the proper channels instead of just going to the store or onto the Internet and buying the part using petty cash.

On the other hand, when she buys the part through the people in the purchasing department, she receives a better price because the department has probably spent a great deal of time negotiating with your supply chain. But by the time she gets the part, you've lost two weeks.

There has to be a sensible balance maintained between the

needs of the creatives and the necessity of process. The company will grind to a stop if it takes three dollars' worth of paperwork and five weeks to buy a ten-cent pencil.

Case in point: During one of my weekly walks around Atari, I spotted a product that was late for our fall trade show. Every week it fell further and further behind. After inquiring about the delay, I found out that the engineer had blown out a critical part—a part that cost fifteen cents.

It turned out that the part was on allocation, meaning that the distributors were out of the large quantities that we usually purchased. Purchasing had simply placed the order and waited—because one of our new managers had told the engineers that they must always go through the purchasing department for parts, with no exceptions. What he had unwittingly done was slow the project down by more than two weeks at a time when the trade show was looming large. Meanwhile, the parts were available at retail just down the street.

This kind of scenario was worse in situations where the part was new and not already entered into our system of regular purchases. Here the purchasing department might enter into prolonged negotiations for quantity purchases before submitting the order for the item, adding a month to the development of new prototypes.

Process isn't bad. Process that hinders growth is bad.

And yet when you hire managers from outside the company, their first instinct is to emulate the process at their old company. You will have to indoctrinate them with the understanding that those old processes are neither necessary nor valuable. This is not easy. It is far more common for people to want to install processes than to loosen them up.

Managers are not evil. They just want to solve problems in a way that keeps the problems from repeating. Unfortunately, the procedures they install can be overly precise and engender some form of hidden cost. As noted, the usual payment for process is loss of personal creativity and speed. Often, the cost of enforcement is greater than the expected savings from the process.

At Atari, almost everyone we hired came from an outfit that operated with more processes than we did. So when new hires wanted to insert more process into our organization, I would always ask, "Why would this speed up our cycle?" This question usually discombobulated them. They were almost always able to answer as to how it might save money. They were seldom able to answer how it would make things go faster.

Today's markets demand speed. Speed trumps all else. It doesn't matter whether you're in marketing, manufacturing, a service industry, or any other business. Given the remarkably fast pace of innovation and change, if you're not focused on speed, you're dead in the water. Creativity without speed is useless. Old rules and standard operating procedures don't lead to innovation.

procedures, they install new technology, analyze and support, train...

I N T R O D U C T I O N
MAKE YOUR WORKPLACE AN ADVERTISEMENT
FOR YOUR COMPANY ADOPT FLEXIBLE PONGS
ADVERTISE CREATIVELY HIRE FOR PASSION
AND INTENSITY IGNORE CREDENTIALS LOOK
FOR HOBBIES USE EMPLOYEES AS RESOURCES
AVOID THE CLONES HIRE THE OBNOXIOUS HIRE
THE CRAZY FIND THE BULLIED LOOK FOR THE
LURKERS ASK ABOUT BOOKS SAIL A BOAT HIRE
UNDER YOUR NOSE COMB THROUGH TWEETS
VISIT CREATIVE COMMUNITIES BEWARE OF
POSEURS ASK ODD QUESTIONS CONDUCT DEEP
INTERVIEWS CELEBRATE INSTITUTE A DEGREE OF
ANARCHY PROMOTE PRANKSTERISM SKUNK IT
UP FOSTER FAIRNESS ISOLATE CHAMPION THE
BAD IDEAS CELEBRATE FAILURE REQUIRE RISK
REWARD TURKEYS MENTOR TREAT EMPLOYEES
AS ADULTS CREATE A CREATIVE CHAIN CREATE
A CREATIVE SPACE DESIGNATE A DEMO DAY
ENCOURAGE ADHD PRELOAD LEARN TO
TALK CREATIVE THINK TOYS NEUTRALIZE THE
NAYSAYERS WRITE DOWN OBJECTIONS TAKE
CREATIVES TO CREATIVE PLACES MAKE SOMETHING
FOR THE RICH CHANGE EVERY DAY, EVERY
HOUR THROW THE DICE DUCK PROCESSES
TAKE A RANDOM WALK THROUGH WIKIPEDIA
DON'T COUNT ON ACCOUNTING INVENT
HAPHAZARD HOLIDAYS MIX IT UP GO TO SLEEP
C O N C L U S I O N

47

Too often, I hear about companies that frown on their employees spending time online. Pay attention to your work! Don't get caught in the Internet trap!

This is wrong.

Your creatives cannot spend all their time focused on the one creative problem you want them to solve. The more their minds are allowed to roam, the more likely their creative juices are to flow (see pong 36).

One of the best ways to do this is to encourage random walks through Wikipedia, the online encyclopedia that has more knowledge stored in it than any place in the world. Think of it as a thesaurus for knowledge. Just as you would look in the thesaurus to find a new and different word than the one you're struggling with, Wikipedia enables you to look up new and different topics around the one you're struggling with.

Say you're thinking about abstract art for a marketing project. You then see a link to visual language, which you've never thought about before. That leads you to Gestalt psychology, which in turn leads you to cybernetics. The next stop is artificial intelligence, and suddenly you see a new way to create an ad campaign based on theories that you hadn't considered until you traveled your random wiki path.

Creativity is seldom quantifiable the way numbers are. Multiple factors enter into any product or project, many of which are obvious but many more are not. If we were talking about quantum mechanics, we'd say there is a cloud of possibilities around any entity. This is also true of ideas. There is a cloud of probabilistic outcomes surrounding every idea, which can be tied to any of its parts, be it its color, shape, functionality, or how it makes you feel.

Sometimes it's the oblique possibilities, the ones on the outer edges of the cloud rather than in the center, that can be most illuminating. You get a new perspective, see the project from different angles, and suddenly paths to completion that had been invisible are now in sight.

Let your creatives open up the clouds of possibilities around any project by encouraging them to walk randomly through Wikipedia, or any other such rabbit hole. In this way, you coax them to examine oblique possibilities and encourage a broader perspective on the issues at hand.

Try it yourself a few times. You'll be surprised at the wealth of ideas a random walk can provide.

Random museum walking

If you are lucky enough to be near the equivalent of a Wikipedia in real life, such as a great museum, take a random walk through it as well.

I learned this trick from Steve Jobs. One day back in the 1980s, I was walking down New York's Fifth Avenue toward the Whitney Museum of American Art when I saw Steve get out of a cab. Although we both knew the other preferred going through museums alone for the freedom of being able to stop or go without any pressure, we decided to walk through the Whitney together.

I quickly discovered that Steve, like me, had found a great deal of creative inspiration at modern art museums. We both liked the truly imaginative pieces but hated those we thought to be glorified junk. The one place where we differed is that Steve liked the very simple stuff. I wanted art to be more complicated. As always, Steve was drawn to elegant simplicity and said that he wanted his entire staff to come back to one particular room where the art was as simple and pure as art can be.

Steve also told me that he had visited The Metropolitan Museum of Art the previous day, and that his notebooks were brimming with ideas to fix the marketing and design of some things he was working on. I never found out the specifics of which pieces of art had inspired these notes. I do know that a random walk through a museum can inspire anyone.

INTRODUCTION
MAKE YOUR WORKPLACE AN ADVERTISEMENT
FOR YOUR COMPANY ADOPT FLEXIBLE PONGS
ADVERTISE CREATIVELY HIRE FOR PASSION
AND INTENSITY IGNORE CREDENTIALS LOOK
FOR HOBBIES USE EMPLOYEES AS RESOURCES
AVOID THE CLONES HIRE THE OBNOXIOUS HIRE
THE CRAZY FIND THE BULLIED LOOK FOR THE
LURKERS ASK ABOUT BOOKS SAIL A BOAT HIRE
UNDER YOUR NOSE COMB THROUGH TWEETS
VISIT CREATIVE COMMUNITIES BEWARE OF
POSEURS ASK ODD QUESTIONS CONDUCT DEEP
INTERVIEWS CELEBRATE INSTITUTE A DEGREE OF
ANARCHY PROMOTE PRANKSTERISM SKUNK IT
UP FOSTER FAIRNESS ISOLATE CHAMPION THE
BAD IDEAS CELEBRATE FAILURE REQUIRE RISK
REWARD TURKEYS MENTOR TREAT EMPLOYEES
AS ADULTS CREATE A CREATIVE CHAIN CREATE
A CREATIVE SPACE DESIGNATE A DEMO DAY
ENCOURAGE ADHD PRELOAD LEARN TO
TALK CREATIVE THINK TOYS NEUTRALIZE THE
NAYSAYERS WRITE DOWN OBJECTIONS TAKE
CREATIVESTOCREATIVEPLACESMAKESOMETHING
FOR THE RICH CHANGE EVERY DAY, EVERY
HOUR THROW THE DICE DUCK PROCESSES
TAKE A RANDOM WALK THROUGH WIKIPEDIA
DON'T COUNT ON ACCOUNTING INVENT
HAPHAZARD HOLIDAYS MIX IT UP GO TO SLEEP
CONCLUSION

48

Creatives always complain about the people in accounting. For the most part, they have good reason to complain. Every now and then you'll run into an accountant who knows there's more to the business than just numbers. Treasure these people, for they are rare.

More typically, the accounting people are genuinely hostile to creativity. This is not an indictment of their personalities or their ability to get along with others, it is simply a reflection of the bean counters' goal: watch the money carefully, and dispense it penuriously. Creativity doesn't interest them. Immediate return on investment does. Try telling an accountant that this terrific new idea of yours will probably bring the company a great deal of money—someday. You just don't know when. Not going to work.

In general, finance departments have more control over the operation of the average company than they should. They are the watchdogs of money. The check doesn't get cut unless they say okay. Sometimes they don't say okay for good reasons. Sometimes they don't say okay for bad reasons. Sometimes they don't say anything because they don't have the proper authorization or paperwork. But they don't tell you any of this. So you wait and wait and wait. For nothing.

I've noticed that people who start their careers in finance are often toxic to innovation. They use financial terms to give themselves gravitas and like to couch a new initiative as being too expensive or financially risky before they've even heard about its specifics. And too often, when a company has problems, the board elevates its CFOs. This is usually not a good solution. If everything is about reducing cost, all new ideas are stillborn.

Because of all this, if there is any one group most likely to stifle the flow of a creative project, it's accounting. (Runners up: the purchasing department and the personnel department.) You need just a few more dollars for that idea of yours to come to fruition, and you need it soon, to beat another company to market. Finance tells you that the budget requires a hold on all payments for a year. You lose.

I'm not saying your company shouldn't have accountants. It should. They're essential parts of any outfit. But make sure that they do their work, the creatives do theirs, and that these two streams run side by side rather than crossing. If accounting plugs up creativity, you've dammed your future.

My advice to accounting: All new projects are financially risky. Get used to it. Figure out how to test and minimize the unknowns. Let the creative juices flow and solve the problems in unexpected ways.

INTRODUCTION
MAKE YOUR WORKPLACE AN ADVERTISEMENT
FOR YOUR COMPANY ADOPT FLEXIBLE PONGS
ADVERTISE CREATIVELY HIRE FOR PASSION
AND INTENSITY IGNORE CREDENTIALS LOOK
FOR HOBBIES USE EMPLOYEES AS RESOURCES
AVOID THE CLONES HIRE THE OBNOXIOUS HIRE
THE CRAZY FIND THE BULLIED LOOK FOR THE
LURKERS ASK ABOUT BOOKS SAIL A BOAT HIRE
UNDER YOUR NOSE COMB THROUGH TWEETS
VISIT CREATIVE COMMUNITIES BEWARE OF
POSEURS ASK ODD QUESTIONS CONDUCT DEEP
INTERVIEWS CELEBRATE INSTITUTE A DEGREE OF
ANARCHY PROMOTE PRANKSTERISM SKUNK IT
UP FOSTER FAIRNESS ISOLATE CHAMPION THE
BAD IDEAS CELEBRATE FAILURE REQUIRE RISK
REWARD TURKEYS MENTOR TREAT EMPLOYEES
AS ADULTS CREATE A CREATIVE CHAIN CREATE
A CREATIVE SPACE DESIGNATE A DEMO DAY
ENCOURAGE ADHD PRELOAD LEARN TO
TALK CREATIVE THINK TOYS NEUTRALIZE THE
NAYSAYERS WRITE DOWN OBJECTIONS TAKE
CREATIVESTOCREATIVEPLACESMAKESOMETHING
FOR THE RICH CHANGE EVERY DAY, EVERY
HOUR THROW THE DICE DUCK PROCESSES
TAKE A RANDOM WALK THROUGH WIKIPEDIA
DON'T COUNT ON ACCOUNTING **INVENT**
HAPHAZARD HOLIDAYS MIX IT UP GO TO SLEEP
CONCLUSION

49

Whenever a corporate culture is thriving, an odd problem can develop. Whereas some companies complain that their employees aren't working hard enough, success can often create a situation in which employees work too hard. And while this might not sound like a problem, it is. Success often creates a culture where people feel driven to create even more success, and more, and more, and then, as the company becomes increasingly known for hiring hard workers, even more. And more.

When people work too hard, they become tired, they make mistakes, they lose their equanimity.

They also lose their perspective, the ability to separate the big problems from the little problems. Everything looks overwhelming, creating tension and anxiety—the enemies of creativity.

Most of all, what distinguishes creatives from other people is their extraordinary judgment. Judgment is a delicate tool, however, and works best when accompanied by sleep, food, and tranquility.

You don't want your creatives to lose judgment. Fatigue myopia is one of the worst things that can happen to an overworked company.

Often, after a trade show or a particularly difficult work period, I would announce, a few days in advance, that on the next Monday or Friday the company would be closed. Besides the fact that they got a day off, employees loved these holidays—even more than those that were part of our planned schedule—because they were unexpected. To add oddness to the gift, I would often pretend to link it to a hero's birthday and announce that we were all taking the day off to celebrate, say, the birth of Blaise Pascal, and suggest that everyone should go learn about him.

There are other ways to surprise and delight your creatives. I once rented a Boeing 727 and flew everyone to Disneyland. It was a chance to forget about being an adult for a day and bond with each other like kids. They had a terrific time.

These days, good companies vie with each other for ways to keep their creatives happy and refreshed. Many Silicon Valley companies buy out a theater for a first-run movie on the midnight before its opening day. Imagination Publishing, a Chicago-based content-marketing agency, offers random company-wide Fridays off, notifying employees through an unexpected email. On one recent fall Monday, the company dismissed employees a few hours early so they could go home and watch the Chicago Bears play. Other companies simply let their employees create their own haphazard holidays, such as content provider Netflix, which gives its people paid, unlimited vacation (and credits the practice with improving both productivity and work/life balance). An estimated 1 percent of American companies have unlimited-vacation policies.

Be creative. Invent holidays whenever the spirit strikes you. Make them specific to your business. If you're an ad agency, let people off if one of your ads goes viral. If you're in technology, think about fewer returns or a total sellout. Let everyone share the joy.

I N T R O D U C T I O N
MAKE YOUR WORKPLACE AN ADVERTISEMENT
FOR YOUR COMPANY ADOPT FLEXIBLE PONGS
ADVERTISE CREATIVELY HIRE FOR PASSION
AND INTENSITY IGNORE CREDENTIALS LOOK
FOR HOBBIES USE EMPLOYEES AS RESOURCES
AVOID THE CLONES HIRE THE OBNOXIOUS HIRE
THE CRAZY FIND THE BULLIED LOOK FOR THE
LURKERS ASK ABOUT BOOKS SAIL A BOAT HIRE
UNDER YOUR NOSE COMB THROUGH TWEETS
VISIT CREATIVE COMMUNITIES BEWARE OF
POSEURS ASK ODD QUESTIONS CONDUCT DEEP
INTERVIEWS CELEBRATE INSTITUTE A DEGREE OF
ANARCHY PROMOTE PRANKSTERISM SKUNK IT
UP FOSTER FAIRNESS ISOLATE CHAMPION THE
BAD IDEAS CELEBRATE FAILURE REQUIRE RISK
REWARD TURKEYS MENTOR TREAT EMPLOYEES
AS ADULTS CREATE A CREATIVE CHAIN CREATE
A CREATIVE SPACE DESIGNATE A DEMO DAY
ENCOURAGE ADHD PRELOAD LEARN TO
TALK CREATIVE THINK TOYS NEUTRALIZE THE
NAYSAYERS WRITE DOWN OBJECTIONS TAKE
CREATIVES TO CREATIVE PLACES MAKE SOMETHING
FOR THE RICH CHANGE EVERY DAY, EVERY
HOUR THROW THE DICE DUCK PROCESSES
TAKE A RANDOM WALK THROUGH WIKIPEDIA
DON'T COUNT ON ACCOUNTING INVENT
HAPHAZARD HOLIDAYS **MIX IT UP** GO TO SLEEP
C O N C L U S I O N

50

One late fall day in 1977, Atari had the kind of problem that most people would envy: too much business. Because we didn't have enough night shift workers to process our Christmas rush orders, we decided that for two weeks every employee was going to have to toil above and beyond his or her normal duties. The plan was for everyone to come in late in the afternoon, do whatever work they needed to do in an hour, and then take over the night shift on the production line.

Those two weeks not only turned out to be a great deal of fun, but also improved our product. On the production line for the first time, the engineers were able to see how their ideas were actually assembled. For instance, it was inefficient to have a screw that took more than three turns to tighten, and yet the engineers discovered that some of their screws required ten or more turns. They fixed that—and made about 150 other changes as well. Meanwhile, the salespeople learned many new ways to sell the product based on what they learned on the line, and sales went up. The accountants were just as sharp and discovered new ways to save money.

Everyone learned to appreciate the manufacturing process as well, because the executives were able to produce only about 70 percent of what the manufacturing line workers made in a shift. Some of the executives had thought the line workers had been loafing, but they soon learned that the workers had developed an economy of motion that the executives couldn't figure out how to reproduce. Everyone gained respect for everyone else, and creativity soared.

Because this experiment was so successful, I've repeated it elsewhere. At Chuck E. Cheese's, for example, everyone had to spend at least three days (sometimes up to a week) making pizza when they first started at the company, and then once a year thereafter.

Try it out. Get your creatives out in the field with the salespeople. Invite your accountants into a creative meeting. Fly your managers to a distant distributor or an underperforming outpost. Oscar Dystel, one of the greatest book publishers in the history of the business, used to ask his editors at Bantam Books to accompany the sales department on its calls to help them expand their sense of the marketplace—and to give the salespeople a chance to tell the editors what they thought of their editorial choices.

INTRODUCTION
MAKE YOUR WORKPLACE AN ADVERTISEMENT
FOR YOUR COMPANY ADOPT FLEXIBLE PONGS
ADVERTISE CREATIVELY HIRE FOR PASSION
AND INTENSITY IGNORE CREDENTIALS LOOK
FOR HOBBIES USE EMPLOYEES AS RESOURCES
AVOID THE CLONES HIRE THE OBNOXIOUS HIRE
THE CRAZY FIND THE BULLIED LOOK FOR THE
LURKERS ASK ABOUT BOOKS SAIL A BOAT HIRE
UNDER YOUR NOSE COMB THROUGH TWEETS
VISIT CREATIVE COMMUNITIES BEWARE OF
POSEURS ASK ODD QUESTIONS CONDUCT DEEP
INTERVIEWS CELEBRATE INSTITUTE A DEGREE OF
ANARCHY PROMOTE PRANKSTERISM SKUNK IT
UP FOSTER FAIRNESS ISOLATE CHAMPION THE
BAD IDEAS CELEBRATE FAILURE REQUIRE RISK
REWARD TURKEYS MENTOR TREAT EMPLOYEES
AS ADULTS CREATE A CREATIVE CHAIN CREATE
A CREATIVE SPACE DESIGNATE A DEMO DAY
ENCOURAGE ADHD PRELOAD LEARN TO
TALK CREATIVE THINK TOYS NEUTRALIZE THE
NAYSAYERS WRITE DOWN OBJECTIONS TAKE
CREATIVESTOCREATIVEPLACESMAKESOMETHING
FOR THE RICH CHANGE EVERY DAY, EVERY
HOUR THROW THE DICE DUCK PROCESSES
TAKE A RANDOM WALK THROUGH WIKIPEDIA
DON'T COUNT ON ACCOUNTING INVENT
HAPHAZARD HOLIDAYS MIX IT UP **GO TO SLEEP**
CONCLUSION

51

Sleep: one of the most essential, most important, most studied functions of the human race. And one of the most ignored by the workplace.

The idea that humans are supposed to stay up all day and then sleep for eight hours through the night is a modern one, invented with the advent of accurate timekeeping, clock-watching bosses, and the mattress industry. For almost all of humankind's history we've actually been polyphasic sleepers: sleeping in multiple periods over a twenty-four-hour stretch. Until recently, humans were at least biphasic, napping during the day and then dozing off again at night.

Yes, we should all get about seven to nine hours of sleep a day, but it doesn't all have to happen in one block. It just has to happen over a twenty-four-hour period.

My sense is that we should all be asleep during at least a small part of the afternoon for the greatest productivity and the clearest minds. Many companies in Japan have long provided facilities for workers to nap. In America, too, forward-thinking companies are installing nap rooms outfitted simply with vinyl pads, offering a darkened space for naps or for workers who want to stay late into the night—or all night—and need a place to crash. Companies such as Cisco Systems, Procter & Gamble, and Google have even purchased EnergyPods—special recliners with pods that block noise and light—so employees can take a nap when they need one.

As I mentioned, Steve Jobs brought a futon to work, and I'd often find him sleeping under his bench. Many of my other creative employees also performed best when allowed to sleep as their bodies desired, rather than as the workday required.

A little proof? A 2004 study published in the journal *Nature* by neuroscientists Ullrich Wagner and Jan Born found that random periods of rapid eye movement (REM) sleep boosted problem-solving skills by 40 percent. A 2009 study by University of California, San Diego sleep guru Sara Mednick and others, published in the *Proceedings of the National Academy of Sciences of the United States of America,* offered similar findings. Additionally, a recent NASA study revealed that a 26-minute nap improved a pilot's performance by 34 percent. Want more? Google "sleep and productivity": you'll get about a million results.

So here's what you need to make sure all your creatives do their best: Beds. Mattresses. Dark rooms. Eye shades. Ear plugs. How much nap time do people require? Individual sleep needs differ. But sleep has five stages: Stage One, Stage Two, slow-wave sleep (SWS, comprising stages three and four), and the fifth stage, REM. Nappers should get at least to Stage Two, the stage that is responsible for increasing alertness and occurs early in the sleep cycle, after two to five minutes of Stage One sleep. To get past this point, you must sleep for much longer. SWS sleep comes after twenty minutes, and REM sleep, which helps enhance memory and perceptual skills, doesn't arrive until later (an entire sleep cycle takes roughly an hour and a half).

I hope this book has not put you to sleep yet. But if it's the middle of the day, that might not be such a bad thing.

INTRODUCTION
MAKE YOUR WORKPLACE AN ADVERTISEMENT
FOR YOUR COMPANY ADOPT FLEXIBLE PONGS
ADVERTISE CREATIVELY HIRE FOR PASSION
AND INTENSITY IGNORE CREDENTIALS LOOK
FOR HOBBIES USE EMPLOYEES AS RESOURCES
AVOID THE CLONES HIRE THE OBNOXIOUS HIRE
THE CRAZY FIND THE BULLIED LOOK FOR THE
LURKERS ASK ABOUT BOOKS SAIL A BOAT HIRE
UNDER YOUR NOSE COMB THROUGH TWEETS
VISIT CREATIVE COMMUNITIES BEWARE OF
POSEURS ASK ODD QUESTIONS CONDUCT DEEP
INTERVIEWS CELEBRATE INSTITUTE A DEGREE OF
ANARCHY PROMOTE PRANKSTERISM SKUNK IT
UP FOSTER FAIRNESS ISOLATE CHAMPION THE
BAD IDEAS CELEBRATE FAILURE REQUIRE RISK
REWARD TURKEYS MENTOR TREAT EMPLOYEES
AS ADULTS CREATE A CREATIVE CHAIN CREATE
A CREATIVE SPACE DESIGNATE A DEMO DAY
ENCOURAGE ADHD PRELOAD LEARN TO
TALK CREATIVE THINK TOYS NEUTRALIZE THE
NAYSAYERS WRITE DOWN OBJECTIONS TAKE
CREATIVES TO CREATIVE PLACES MAKE SOMETHING
FOR THE RICH CHANGE EVERY DAY, EVERY
HOUR THROW THE DICE DUCK PROCESSES
TAKE A RANDOM WALK THROUGH WIKIPEDIA
DON'T COUNT ON ACCOUNTING INVENT
HAPHAZARD HOLIDAYS MIX IT UP GO TO SLEEP
CONCLUSION

52

"The best way to predict the future is to invent it."
—Computer scientist Alan Kay

If you can fix your company's bureaucracy, if you can streamline your creative chain, if you can establish a workplace where innovation is rewarded and naysayers are denied power, if you can celebrate, if you can play with toys, if you can follow many of the other pongs in this book, you may well be fashioning a workplace that cultivates creativity. In that case, the next Steve Jobs may already be applying for a position at your company.

You might even find that the next Steve Jobses are already working for you—although if that's the case, the odds are good that they're wilting under your company's hierarchy, their inspiration destroyed by your management team, by the lack of support for their ideas, by the fear that taking a risk will lead to being fired, and so on.

As mentioned, it isn't enough to find the next Steve Jobses and hire them; you have to create a situation in which they can flourish, and then your company can, too.

Remember that Steve's own board at Apple eventually fired him. The reason? They thought they could not control what they considered to be all his crazy projects. So even Steve Jobs lost out to the supposedly sophisticated managers of Apple—which promptly tanked until Steve was brought in again to lead the company back to success.

If you are able to abide by many of the pongs in this book, you, too, will be on your way to success. However, there's one last pong to keep in mind. It's a simple one:

Act!

Everyone who has ever taken a shower has had a good idea. The thing that matters is what you do with that idea once you get out of the shower. So if there's only one thing you take from this book, it's this: You must act! Do something! Too many people read books, listen to lectures, attend seminars, and then return to their lives without changing a thing. If that's how you respond to this book, then I've failed. Because it isn't enough to understand that you must find, hire, and nurture creative people, you must actually go out and *do* it.

You and your company are in a daily battle with the future—blink, and your competitor may suddenly take a giant step forward, leaving you wondering what happened. Blink, and your competitor may have taken over your market, and it's too late for you to do anything about it. The future can leap out at you from any direction—do you think that Nokia or BlackBerry ever thought their business would be decimated by a California-based computer company named after a fruit that had never before entered the cell phone market?

You must be of the future, not the past. If you're truly creative, you can actually help dictate that future. Being creative means making the future happen faster—and having some control over it as well.

All the companies that are known for being innovative act. They do things—many things. If you want to have a good idea, great, have lots of good ideas. But if you want to be successful, act on as many of those ideas as you can. Some will fail and the world will quickly forget about them, but the ones that succeed can change the trajectory of your business and transport you to new heights.

This is one of the traits I admired most about the original Steve Jobs: He acted. In fact, he never stopped acting. He was constantly tackling new ideas, putting new concepts into play, looking for the next big thing. Much of Apple's success has been due to his frenetic activity.

It was always that way. For example, in the early 1980s, I invited Steve to Chuck E. Cheese's to see some of our research projects. We had just started our Kadabrascope division to investigate computer-aided animation; it consisted of a few software engineers and a couple of animators working on a VAX 11-750 (a hot minicomputer at the time). Steve was very interested in the project and we talked for hours about how the future of animation was computer aided, although we knew we weren't there yet.

The VAX 11-750 used a Unix operating system, which Steve later put on his NeXT personal computer and as mentioned in Pong 31, could run multiple software programs.

Several years later, right after the Christmas holidays, Steve showed up at my home in Woodside. He wanted to talk more about computer-aided animation—a continuation of the same conversation we'd had years ago, which says something about his focus. He was especially curious about my opinion of the Lucas division of Pixar, namely its animation technology.

I told him that we were reaching the break point, that point at which the technology was ready for commercialization on a larger scale, but still might be risky. After all, no one had yet used computer-based animation successfully for full-length cartoons. Once they did, I predicted, it would become the prevailing technology.

Steve replied that since he'd left Apple (temporarily, as noted above), he had been fascinated with Pixar's work in this area and was thinking of investing in the company. I told him that his nose for such things was excellent and that he should do what he always does: "Act!" I said. "And then solve any problems that come along."

He thanked me and we talked about other things. Only a few months later, I found out that he had gone out and made a significant investment in Pixar.

Sometime later, I received an invitation to the San Francisco premiere of the movie *Toy Story*. At the party afterward, we talked about how terrific the animation technology was.

"Great work, Jobs," I said.

He smiled. "I acted," he said, and moved off into the crowd.

ACKNOWLEDGMENTS

Many people have helped me throughout my life, but there isn't room to name them all. I would, however, like to single out the following people for their support.

My wife Nancy, who has been a constant calming influence in my otherwise chaotic life.

My parents, who allowed me to put a red-and-white-striped antenna pole on the roof of our house.

My kids, who have kept me young and pushed the boundaries of creativity in their own way.

Alissa, my oldest daughter and the best publicist I've ever found.

My third grade teacher, Mrs. Cook, who set me on my path with her magic science box in the closet.

Bob Noyce, who was my mentor.

Al Alcorn, who was the real inventor of *Pong*.

Steve Mayer, who was the chief architect of the 2600.

Mike Hatcher, who was the puppeteer and producer of all the Chuck E. Cheese's shows.

My in-laws, for their many years of unwavering support and friendship.

Peter Sprague, who has been a constant friend through thick and thin.

Ted Dabney, the best founding partner I could have hoped for.

Tim Sanders, who is the best tour guide for the new world of publishing.

All those who helped me with my research, including Nick Bromley, Matt Corkins, Tetsuhiko Endo, Simon Geballe, Michael Pinchera, Adam Wren, and especially Miranda Spencer.

And finally, Gene Stone, who has the extraordinary ability to put my jumbled thoughts into eloquent words.

Answers to questions on page 81

1. The three women are beauty-contest finalists just after the winner has been announced.

2. The numbers are in alphabetical order.

3. The dates are B.C., not A.D.

4. His breath.

5. Dorothy. Her friends are the Cowardly Lion (animal), the Scarecrow (vegetable), and the Tin Man (mineral).

ABOUT THE AUTHORS

Nolan Bushnell (www.nolanbushnell.com) is a technology pioneer, entrepreneur and engineer. Often cited as the father of the video-game industry, he is best known as the founder of Atari Corporation and Chuck E. Cheese's Pizza Time Theater. Over the past four decades he has founded numerous companies, including Catalyst Technologies, the first technology incubator; Etak, the first digital navigation system; ByVideo, the first online ordering system; and uWink, the first touchscreen menu ordering and entertainment system, among others.

Currently, with his new company, Brainrush, he is devoting his talents to enhancing and improving the educational process by integrating the latest developments in brain science. Additionally, he enjoys motivating and inspiring others in his speeches on entrepreneurship, creativity, innovation, and education.

Gene Stone (www.genestone.com), a former book, magazine, and newspaper editor for such companies as the *Los Angeles Times,* *Esquire*, Harcourt Brace, and Simon & Schuster, has ghostwritten thirty books (many of which were *New York Times* bestsellers) for a wide range of people in many different fields. Stone has also written numerous titles under his own name, including *The Secrets of People Who Never Get Sick*, which has been translated into more than twenty languages; the #1 *New York Times* bestseller *Forks Over Knives;* and *The Watch,* the definitive book on the wristwatch.